PROCOL HARUM

PROCOL HARUM

Beyond The Pale

Claes Johansen

SAF Publishing Ltd

SAF Publishing Ltd

First published in 2000 by SAF Publishing Ltd.

SAF Publishing Ltd.
Unit 7, Shaftesbury Centre,
85 Barlby Road,
London. W10 6BN
ENGLAND

ISBN 0 946719 28 4

A CIP catalogue record for this book is available from the British Library.

Printed in England by The Cromwell Press, Trowbridge, Wiltshire.

Acknowledgements

Thanks to:

Matthew Fisher, Gary Brooker, Keith Reid, Robin Trower, David Knights, BJ Wilson (wherever you are), Mick Grabham, Chris Copping, Dave Ball, Ray Royer, Bobby Harrison, Mick Brownlee, Richard Brown, Garry Nicholls, John Kalinowski, Bob Lloyd, John Denton, Wilko Johnson, Mickey Jupp, Steve Hyams, Les Lambert, Henry Myers, Bernie Tormé, Henry Scott-Irvine, Tony Catchpole, Alan Bown, Geoff Bannister, Stan Halden, Paul Carter, Derek Reid, Colin Crosby, Mike Lease, Steve Shirley, Kenny White, Mike Roberts, David Wells (Tenth Planet Records), Bill Allerton (Stand Out, London), Phil Smee (Strange Things Archive), Linda Fisher, Franky Brooker, Chris Briggs (Chrysalis), Keith Duncan, Diane Rolph & John Grayson (*Shine On*), Mick Fish, Chris Welch, Ole Knudsen, Stig Nielsen, Mac Poole, Ray Fenwick, Mike Gott (BGO), John Reed (Sequel), Clive Zone, Sarah Lees (Castle), Tony Rounce (Westside), Steve Davis and David Burton (EMI), Repertoire Records, Tom McKee (Endangered Records) and Angel Air.

... and to the photographers:
Jan Persson, Robin Copping, Peder Bundgaard and Nik Kalinowski.

Also thanks to those helpful souls with their big red pens, kind ears, encouraging remarks and incredible patience: Jim Hart, Michelle & Gareth Taborn (of Second Spin, Barnstable), Sam Cameron, Roland Clare, Peter Purnell, my wife Tine and my daughter Sandra.
  I'd be nowhere without you.

Contents

Introduction

Because I grew up in Scandinavia, I grew up with Procol Harum. They were always there, ever since "A Whiter Shade Of Pale" hit in 1967 (and in a sense even before that – Copenhagen was a stronghold for Procol Harum forerunners The Paramounts, who for periods were a standing attraction at the notorious Hit House). What I remember even more vividly is "A Salty Dog" being played constantly on the radio throughout the summer of 1969. I was eleven years old, played a bit of piano myself, and had just started to learn English. This was music made for me. It was like nothing I had ever heard before. It sucked me in.

Later, in my teenage years, Procol Harum became the first group I saw playing "live" and whose records I systematically collected. They were the main reason why I bought a record player. They were the main reason why I started playing in groups. On a less positive note, they were the reason why I tried in vain to grow a moustache.

This book, of course, had to start with a dream.

I dreamed I was writing a book about Procol Harum and when I woke up I knew it was going to happen. What the dream didn't tell me was that it would take more than fifteen years to get it right.

This dream came to me sometime in early 1983. Soon after, I packed a suitcase and went to England where I interviewed Matthew Fisher. That proved to be a miraculous starting point. Matt was not only keen to help me in any way he could, he also had all the connections, the addresses and phone numbers I needed. Even more importantly, the sheer mention of his name seemed to be the key that could unlock any door.

So, soon after, I found myself interviewing Gary Brooker, Keith Reid, Robin Trower, Mick Grabham and David Knights. The following year I met BJ Wilson in Denmark, when he was touring with Joe Cocker.

An advert in *New Musical Express* put me in touch with another Procol Harum fan, Bob Lloyd in Australia. I sent Bob a list of questions and on my behalf he interviewed Chris Copping and Dave Ball, who to our amazement turned out to live practically just around the corner from him. Thanks Bob!

So for a while it seemed that fate was with us. But in the late 1980s, when I wrote the first part of my Procol Harum biography, it was met with no interest on the publishing front.

I moved to England with my family in 1992 and since then worked for several record companies writing sleeve-notes for compact disc releases (I also consolidated my career as a writer in Denmark with what today amounts to fourteen books, most of them novels). Coincidentally, quite a few of these CDs had Procol Harum connections. That was how I got to know Ray Royer, Bobby Harrison and people like Mike Lease (who worked closely with producer Denny Cordell during the mid-sixties). I also stayed in touch with most of the other past and present members of the band, occasionally updating my interview material and discussing with them all things Harum.

In the meantime general interest in the group was obviously increasing, perhaps as a result of the 1991 reunion. Suddenly there were fanzines, magazine and newspaper articles, new releases, tours, gigs, and a Website on the Internet with more than 1100 pages of solid Harum information.

In the autumn of 1998 I started approaching publishers again with a view to completely rewriting and finishing my original manuscript. This time I was met with considerably more interest.

It would be wrong of me to deny the difficulties I have encountered during the writing of this book. Most surprisingly, when I informed Keith Reid and Gary Brooker that the biography was now finally going ahead they showed no interest in continuing to assist me with my work. Hence the whole concept of the book had to be reconsidered at a very awkward stage, and though my initial interviews with both of them were very comprehensive much time still had to be spent on checking facts through other sources.

Another problem has been the overwhelming amount of material. This book covers more than forty years of musical and biographical history, so for obvious reasons it has been necessary to focus on certain periods rather than others. I have mainly concentrated my efforts on what I see as the most important artistic contributions made by the group – their first six albums, recorded from 1967 to 1971. To my mind Procol Harum around 1972 – like, indeed, the main bulk of rock bands at the time – went from making music that was truly great by any standard to releasing records which primarily sounded good at the time. However, that doesn't mean the group's later years (nor The Paramounts' illustrious career during the Beat Boom) is neglected, as during these periods Gary Brooker and his cohorts still produced the occasional excellent and sometimes even classic record.

Hopefully, the reader will find that I have managed to get the balance right.

Claes Johansen, Devon 1999

Part One

Beginnings, 1945–1966

How the tale unfolds

The first time I ever heard rhythm 'n' blues was when I was walking down the corridor at school one day. There was a grand piano which used to stand there. I hear some music and someone playing and singing 'What'd I Say'. I'd never heard this song, I was a little bit young then for rock 'n' roll. I thought, "That's great!" And that was Gary Brooker...

Wilko Johnson

Even if Gary Brooker had never met lyricist Keith Reid and formed Procol Harum, even if he had never written a single note in all his life and his career had ground to a halt in the autumn of 1966 – which in fact very nearly happened – he would still be highly regarded today as the singer and piano player in one of Britain's finest rhythm 'n' blues combos, The Paramounts. This was the first group Brooker toured and recorded with.

Gary Brooker was born on 29 May 1945 in Hackney, London, but spent the first nine years of his life mainly in Bush Hill Park, Middlesex. It was a musical upbringing. Brooker still speaks fondly of his father, Harry, who was the Hawaiian guitarist in Felix Mendelssohn's Hawaiian Serenaders, an entertainment orchestra of some renown in the 1940s and 1950s.

The piano was Gary's preferred instrument right from the start. At the age of five he was given lessons by a woman teacher with the unfortunate habit of hitting her pupils over the fingers with her pen. No wonder the boy didn't feel particularly motivated, but for a while his family encouraged him to continue. Sometimes at informal gatherings, such as private parties, Harry would suggest his son come up and join him on a few numbers. Gary Brooker still recalls having his stage debut at the tender age of seven.

In 1954 the family moved to Southend-on-Sea, a seaside resort on the east coast of England between Harwich and Dover, and for a while the lessons stopped. Two years later, Harry Brooker died. The following year Gary started going to a local music teacher called Ronald Meachem, who would have a profound influence on his approach to the piano.

Instead of starting his pupils off on the *Academy Beginner's Book*, which appears to have been the norm for piano tutors at the time, Mr Meachem would guide his pupils through the process of analyzing chord structures and scales, explaining exactly what was going on in an enticing and enthusiastic manner.

This in itself was advanced for the day, but Ronald Meachem went further than that. Gary Brooker's recollection of how the two of them went through a "boogie phase" together nearly says it all. This was a teacher who didn't detach himself from his pupils, nor did he shun modern popular music with its formal simplicity.

More than anything else Mr Meachem seems to have induced self-confidence in his pupils. Gary Brooker started his first group at the age of twelve (initially playing banjo and guitar, then switching to piano). He was at that time a student at Westcliff High School and the other members were all friends of his.

John Denton, a long-standing fan of The Paramounts and later on himself a piano player with Wilko Johnson's Solid Senders, went to school with Gary Brooker:

"I was a year younger than Gary, and Wilko was a year younger than me. For me Westcliff High School For Boys, during 1958-1963, was a dark, cold, unsympathetic place. It thought it was a public school. It seemed obsessed with Rugby football, took pride in its new science block and had little time for those pupils of an artistic bent. Rock 'n' roll was dismissed as puerile. Some of us would congregate in the Art room with acoustic guitars, CND badges and a plug-in Dansette record player. That's when I first heard Ray Charles' 'Sticks

And Stones'. I recall the music teacher roundly scorning a Buddy Holly song; he would play us Elgar's 'Enigma Variations' on his record player. Nothing wrong with Elgar, but the mood was a grimly serious one. I'd say that any musical interest Gary had must have evolved in opposition to that institution, not as a result of any positive input whatsoever."

Brooker's first band were called The Electrics. Since this was the late 1950s they were, of course, a skiffle group. They gigged at private gatherings such as weddings. For a fee of just £1 you could hire this line-up, which included Gary's school friend Grahame Derrick, also known as "Diz".

After a while the group was augmented with a lead singer. The other members were now all around thirteen or fourteen, their new front man some six years older with a visual likeness to Billy Fury. However, the line-up didn't last long and for a while Brooker was in another local group who played mainly Les Paul inspired material. After a short while his lack of enthusiasm for this particular kind of repertoire led him to leave and join Johnny Short and the Coasters instead, who were so blatantly in awe of their American idols that they had directly copied their name.

Johnny Short was the group's guitarist, a keen follower of Carl Perkins. Ironically – since the American Coasters were a vocal group – Johnny's repertoire contained mainly instrumentals. An incident none of them were ever likely to forget took place at a local gig. Gary Brooker:

"I remember setting my piano on fire one night at the Leigh Yacht Club. I left a cigarette on the end, and the celluloid on the keys caught fire and flared. The flames got up to 'a' below middle 'c' before I poured a pint over it!"[1]

Not long afterwards a band contest was to take place at the Palace Hotel Dance Hall in Southend. This particular occasion would prove fateful for Brooker. Johnny Short and the Coasters didn't win the competition (a group called Mickey Law and the Outlaws did, though it was claimed that someone had fixed the votes – Johnny's lot came in second). However, this was the occasion where Gary Brooker was spotted by another young local musician – guitarist Robin Trower.

Like most other members of The Paramounts and Procol Harum over the years, Robin Trower emphasises his working-class roots although his father was in fact self-employed. "He worked very hard and I think he made it possible for us to live perhaps a little bit better than most working-class people were at the time," Trower told me.

The family originally lived in London but moved to the countryside during the very late part of the Second World War. This was where Robin, their second son, was born on 7 March 1945.

Over the following years there were a number of significant upheavals in the boy's life. The family emigrated to Canada for a while, and then to New Zealand. When Robin was seven years old they returned to England. In the meantime his paternal grandmother had moved to Southend, so that seemed like an appropriate place to settle.

From the outset Gary Brooker and Robin Trower had one thing in common – both had their early lives overshadowed by the loss of one of their parents. In Robin's case it was the mother. His father remarried, and if there was any significant love of music in Trower's childhood home it came from his stepmother. Trower recalls:

"She was very keen on Rogers & Hammerstein, *Kismet* and *South Pacific* and stuff like that. But it was really my older brother that started bringing American records home, and Elvis – that sort of thing. That's what really got me hooked on it. I wanted to be like Elvis. That would be about 1959 because I recall getting a guitar for Christmas when I was fourteen."

The first person to teach Robin Trower a few rudimentary guitar chords was a friend from school, Chris Copping. He was learning classical piano so he knew a bit of theory, and he and Trower formed their first group together. On at least one or two occasions they appear to have called themselves The Raiders. Chris Copping played a guitar that was tuned down to emulate the sound of a bass. Their lead vocalist was Robin Trower's older brother Mick, and the drummer was schoolmate Garry Nicholls.

It was at the 1960 Palace Hotel Dance Hall competition in Southend where, according to Gary Brooker, several important decisions were made during the evening. One was based on the fact that Robin Trower was extremely keen to enhance The Raiders' line-up with a pianist, thereby emulating his heroes, a group from nearby Romford called The Rockerfellas who were slightly older and more experienced than The Raiders and big heroes among the youth of Southend.

From the audience The Raiders, who also participated in the competition, were watching Johnny Short and the Coasters blasting away on stage. Robin Trower and Chris Copping were particularly impressed with their piano player, so after the gig they got in touch with Johnny Short, who was naïve enough to provide them with Gary Brooker's address. Little did Johnny realise at the time that he was giving away his pianist as well.

The other important thing that reportedly happened at the Palace Hotel Dance Hall competition was that an idea came to the mind of local entrepreneur Peter Martin to form some kind of a Southend "supergroup". This group would contain members from bands that were all competing that night – The Raiders, Johnny Short and the Coasters, Bob Scott and the Clansmen, and Mickey Law and the Outlaws.

The first step on the route to forming such a band came when Trower and Copping called on Gary Brooker to suggest he join The Raiders. Brooker accepted on condition that he could remain a member of the Coasters as well. For some time after that Gary would do occasional gigs with The Raiders, and likewise Chris Copping stood in on bass for the Coasters who didn't have a regular bass player.

Then The Raiders split up. Eventually, drummer Garry Nicholls joined The Monotones, who released a handful of singles on Pye in 1964-65; before joining Peter & the Wolves. Meanwhile Robin Trower and Chris Copping asked drummer Mick Brownlee to join them in a new band. Brownlee had previously been in Mickey Law and the Outlaws.

The three of them started rehearsing in the front room of Robin Trower's father's house in Lancaster Garden, Southend. In between numbers they would discuss how to get Gary Brooker to join them on a permanent basis, and what the name of their new group should be.

One day Robin Trower called Gary Brooker on the phone to tell him about a gig the band had booked for the following Saturday. As always, he suggested Brooker come along.

Gary Brooker replied that it was impossible for him to go to the gig; he had already promised to play another job with Johnny Short on the same date. Having decided that in a situation like this the Coasters would come before Robin Trower's band that was the end of the matter as far as the pianist was concerned. Gary Brooker claims that

Robin Trower explained that he had already spoken with Johnny
Short, who had told him that The Coasters' gig was cancelled. Still
according to Brooker, Johnny Short had not spoken to Robin Trower
and in fact the Coasters gig *wasn't* cancelled. Consequently, Johnny
Short came to the conclusion that since Gary Brooker hadn't shown
up he must have decided to leave the group. Whatever the case may
be, Brooker was now a full-time member of Robin Trower's band.

One day they were sitting together with manager Peter Martin, once
again debating the name problem. Leafing through a magazine they
stumbled upon a reference to Paramount Productions, the famous
American film company. Everyone thought it sounded like a good
name for a group, so from that moment on they became The
Paramounts.

For the first few months The Paramounts were backing lead singer
Brian Richards, but since he rarely showed up at gigs he was soon
replaced by Bob Scott. This seems to have happened sometime in
early 1961, and thus Peter Martin's "Southend supergroup project"
had become a fact.

Bob Scott was a fine singer with a voice not unlike that of Ricky
Nelson. The group played some of Nelson's hits and also songs made
famous by Elvis Presley and Jerry Lee Lewis. Generally they were
covering songs by US groups with a rock 'n' roll or rhythm 'n' blues
style. This was pretty advanced for a young British group at a time
when the closest BBC Radio would ever come to this kind of music
was the odd recording by Cliff Richard and the Shadows.

The early Paramounts were no strangers to the Shadows' repertoire
either, covering hit records such as "F.B.I.". But whatever they were
playing they were obviously pretty good at it, and they swiftly moved
from gigging at private parties to performing at dance hall venues and
US air bases.

One night the group was ready to go on stage but Bob Scott had
failed to turn up. There was panic in the dressing-room and Robin
Trower suggested Gary Brooker take over the microphone. Trower
still had the image of The Rockerfellas in the back of his mind, and
since their lead singer was also their pianist it made sense to him that
Brooker should become the singer of The Paramounts.

Gary Brooker failed to see the reasoning. He wasn't that keen on
The Rockerfellas, and furthermore his singing career so far had been

more-or-less confined to the bathroom of his mother's house. All in all he was more than reluctant to take up the challenge. Then Chris Copping suddenly hit him in his soft spot by saying, "Come on, Gary. You can be like Ray Charles." Finally, the pianist surrendered and, clearing his throat, went out to greet his audience for the first time as a lead singer.

By all accounts it didn't work particularly well. Initially Brooker hadn't much control over his voice, and for a while the singing was split between himself and drummer Mick Brownlee. The important thing, however, was that Bob Scott never returned to the group, and from then on they were primarily a self-contained four-piece unit.

No Money Down

The Paramounts were the best R&B band I have seen and ever will see! They were shit hot! They were magic! I used to go to the Shades Club every time they played. I wouldn't mind going back twenty years just to go down there again!

Mickey Jupp in 1984

Over the following months Gary Brooker's singing started to improve rapidly and he obviously enjoyed his new role immensely. Mick Brownlee was out of the group for a while and different people were sitting in for him, like The Raiders' old drummer Garry Nicholls, Tony Diamond (previously with The Red Diamonds, later in Mickey Jupp's band The Orioles), and Bobby Harrison, a relation of The Rockerfellas' pianist/singer Tony Sumner – and at a much later stage the drummer in early Procol Harum.

On a personal level The Paramounts had arrived at the stage where they were leaving school and had to decide what to do with their lives in general. Gary Brooker went on to Southend Municipal College to study Zoology and Botany. Robin Trower started working with his brother cleaning windows. They both carried on playing in the band, but Chris Copping was doing well academically and started having general doubts about the future of British rhythm 'n' blues.

"At this stage no one had heard of The Beatles yet," he told Bob Lloyd in 1984. "I had classical piano lessons as a child, but I wasn't good enough to take it up as a career. Modern jazz appealed to me, but a few aspects scared me. It seemed like all the good jazz musicians I was into were either junkies or alcoholics, and some of the really good ones were a mixture of both. I thought I'd better stick to the straight and narrow, and so I didn't become either a junkie or an alcoholic until, well, quite a bit later."

For a while Ada Baggerly, who was also in the Orioles, would stand in on bass, until Copping finally made up his mind and left The Paramounts in order to go to university.

Soon afterwards Grahame "Diz" Derrick, Gary Brooker's old school friend and former fellow-member of The Electrics, joined as a bass player on a steady basis. With Mick Brownlee back in the fold and Peter Martin safely in control of all the bookings The Paramounts played on through 1961-62. Some gigs they would do on their own, at other times they were hired as a backing band for visiting artists such as Ricky Valance and Tommy Bruce, performing a series of shows on the ferry to Calais under the banner of *Rock Across The Channel*. This was quite a prestigious occasion which included other musical legends such as The Shadows, Duffy Power and the Dreamers, and Gerry and the Pacemakers.

There weren't many rehearsals before these gigs. The band would be provided with rudimentary charts of the songs, instructing them which chords they were supposed to play. Then the "stars" would turn up briefly before they were due to go on, and optimistically expect everything to go right. Fees were virtually non-existent but by all accounts it was good fun and excellent practice.

What The Paramounts were really into, however, was playing the kind of material that was closest to their hearts, particularly black American R&B. In fact, more records in this genre were released in the UK than is normally assumed, but the pressings were usually extremely small in numbers. It was very much a specialist's scene, and these records were never heard on the radio. Likewise, they weren't normally available in record shops in provincial towns like Southend.

Consequently, bands like The Paramounts depended greatly on local people who were "in the know" – collectors with an impeccable taste in black American music. One such collector who played an immensely important role in creating the group's repertoire was Tony

Wilkinson, who also supplied the jukebox in the Shades Club in Southend.

This particular jukebox was pivotal in the history of The Paramounts, but even more important was the Shades Club itself which was located underneath the Penguin Café on the Southend Seafront. In 1961 Robin Trower's entrepreneurial father, Len, had bought the establishment following a local scandal where its previous proprietor had been accused of stealing money from his charity collection boxes.

The members of The Paramounts used to frequent the café, debating future plans over tea and fizzy drinks. One day it suddenly dawned on them that they could perhaps turn the basement underneath the café into a club of some kind. As they descended the stairs to the cellar they realised that it was already occupied by plastic penguins which presumably had been used by the previous owner for advertising purposes. Luckily, it turned out that these creatures were highly flammable and it didn't take long before soaring clouds of black smoke over the area signalled the fact that plastic penguins were now an extinct species on the Southend seafront. Next came the job of painting and decorating the room, purchasing a piano and building a stage. A few weeks later the club was ready to open.

According to legend, roadie John "Kellogs" Kalinowski was one day "found behind the jukebox in the Shades". He had been a steady customer from the days before Len Trower bought the place and still recalls the Penguin Café as having by far the best pin-ball machine in Southend.

It was around this time that the phenomenon of the rivalry between Mods versus Rockers was starting to happen. Gary Brooker has always been particularly careful to clarify that The Paramounts, though their repertoire must have been a godsend to local scooter boys, were completely impartial in this pointless gang struggle. They played music for people who liked rhythm 'n' blues, no matter what they preferred to call themselves. Nevertheless, the Shades soon became a bit of a Mod "hang-out".

In the liner-notes for *Whiter Shades Of R&B*, a Paramounts compilation LP released by Edsel records in 1983, John Denton gave the following description of the Shades Club:

"It cost a shilling to descend into the dimly-lit cavernous room, formed of two dark areas fronted by a small dancing space and a low stage. Behind the stage, a zany mural depicted The Paramounts' cartoon replicas. In the two back chambers one could perceive youths sipping cola, while girls danced effortlessly to the jukebox sound of 'Thumbin' A Ride'. The dance area was to fill as The Paramounts plugged in and commenced to rock. Egg boxes bedecked the walls and ceiling, serving as primitive sound proofing; the cluster of 'backing vocalist' fans was so effective in this environment despite the throbbing sound; the people around the stage were executing what would be termed the Pogo some fifteen years later. This was the most exciting music I'd ever heard."

The group now felt it was time to go professional. The only problem was that Mick Brownlee was about to get married and needed a more steady job in order to provide for a young family. So he quit to become a bricklayer instead, leaving the rest of the band to seek out a new drummer.

Mick Brownlee was an excellent musician and replacing him wasn't going to be easy. There were no immediate local alternatives available, so The Paramounts advertised in the national music paper, *Melody Maker*, with the perhaps somewhat optimistic call for a drummer to join a "professional group".

Auditions were held in Orpington, Kent. One of the candidates was a certain Barrie James Wilson from Edmonton, North London. He didn't look like much, a skinny fellow with arms like spaghetti. Could he really play the drums? It turned out that he fitted the bill superbly, so "BJ" was quickly accepted.

Born 18 March 1947 Barrie James Wilson had started playing drums as a member of the Boys' Brigade. Here he picked up certain attitudes which (like his idol in years to come, The Who's Keith Moon) he would occasionally incorporate in a tongue-in-cheek manner into the rock music idiom. His stepfather was a postman, and his mother worked as a cleaner.

At school Barrie was approached by Les Lambert and Tony Jones, who played guitar and bass respectively, and who wanted to form a group. After a while Tony Jones was replaced by Alan Cartwright (then known by his middle name, George). Remarkably, all these people can later be found somewhere in the history of Procol Harum.

According to Les Lambert, BJ Wilson got himself into serious trouble at school:

"He had this rebel image, you see. We were sixteen at the time and they had this book where pupils got their names written into if they were caught smoking. If you got caught a certain number of times you were in trouble. Barrie was caught once too often so he somehow managed to make his way into the room where this book was being kept. He took the book away and tried setting fire to it out in one of the toilets but then I think he panicked and dropped the book into the toilet and tried to flush it. They caught him and he got chucked out of school."

It wasn't long after this untimely departure from the education system that BJ Wilson spotted The Paramounts' advert in *Melody Maker*. Kenny White:

"He was nervous about going and asked me if I would go along with him. So I did. We caught the bus, Barrie with his snare drum under his arm – still no case and his sticks in his pocket. There in a small hall we met, and he auditioned for, The Paramounts. He got the job."[2]

Soon after, BJ Wilson moved to Southend. Since he had come directly from London and had no place to stay, he simply moved into the Shades Club where Robin Trower was living permanently as well.

"When I joined The Paramounts I'd never heard music like it," BJ Wilson told me. "I'd never heard rhythm 'n' blues very much, apart from Chuck Berry and a few of the more popular things. It was a real musical eye-opener for me to hear BB King and Ray Charles. Just really obscure things that you never heard anywhere else in England at the time. There were very few people doing that sort of thing. Most of the groups were playing Shadows music and Cliff Richard – real pop stuff."

BJ Wilson became a member of The Paramounts in the late summer of 1963. During the following year the group's career would change drastically. From being a minor local act playing small clubs, dance halls and American air bases they became caught up in the so-called Beat Boom, gigging with The Rolling Stones and The Beatles, releasing records for a major label and playing on national television shows.

Stay tuned ...

Two steps from the blues

Peter Martin told us to record 'Poison Ivy'. I said, 'That's sacred stuff!' If we'd had the choice we wouldn't have made a record at all!

Gary Brooker [3]

Right from the early days the individual talents of all four Paramounts were evident, and likewise their personalities. People in and around the band describe Gary Brooker as laid-back and easy-going, sometimes to an extent where there were complaints about his reluctance to participate in unpleasant but necessary tasks, such as packing the equipment into the van after gigs. Obviously extremely talented and destined for greater things, Brooker was particularly fond of Ray Charles songs and, a little later on, sweet soul material.

For Robin Trower, who was more of a straight blues man, this wasn't always satisfying. He actually once left the stage in the Shades Club during a Ray Charles song, not angry but just frustrated with this kind of material which didn't allow him to play in his favoured style. Likewise, Mick Brownlee told me of a discussion the group once had about including a certain Shadows instrumental in their repertoire. Trower ended the debate by simply packing up his gold-plated Gretsch Country Gent guitar and leaving the room. He seems to have been the group's most ambitious and determined member, his whole life centred on his love for black American music.

BJ Wilson, being the youngest in the group, appears to have adopted the role of everyone's little brother – humorous and loveable, generally having a laugh at the world. Followers of the band recall him as enigmatic, but also highly strung at times, and slower to mature than the other members.

Bass player Diz Derrick was probably the most versatile member. Once when Gary Brooker failed to show up at a gig at the Shades Club, Derrick just sat down at the piano and played all the same songs that Brooker normally played. Only his singing seems to have let the group down on that occasion, where by some accounts Chris Copping stood in on bass (the only time he and BJ Wilson actually played together in The Paramounts).

The Paramounts went professional in August 1963. Gary Brooker describes how there had already been two attempts to start their recording career:

"We'd been up to London before with a woman from Leigh-on-Sea, who had a lot of money and an eye for young fellows. She got us into a studio in London, but nothing came of it."[4]

The band's second attempt in the studio was more successful and produced a demo single containing a version of "Poison Ivy" on the A-side, and on the flip a cover of a more down-to-earth R&B classic, "Further On Up The Road". This single was made for promotional purposes only and just five or six acetate copies were cut. It was recorded at IBC Studios and engineered by Glyn Johns (later a world-class producer for The Who and many others). With their straightforward, dry and raw production these two sides heralded a promising start for The Paramounts on the recording front, and on the back of the demo they signed to EMI.

By now the Beat Boom had started with the arrival of The Beatles, and little combos up and down the country were suddenly churning out rhythm 'n' blues covers like there was no tomorrow. For The Paramounts, who had been performing such material for several years, it was a strange experience no longer to feel alone in covering songs by Chuck Berry and Little Richard.

To keep their exclusive status the group moved on to covering slightly more obscure artists like Bobby Bland, whose 1961 LP *Two Steps From The Blues* became a big influence on them. At the same time a lot of the poppier material had to go, though Buddy Holly always remained a favourite. The Paramounts' live set included at least three songs made famous by Holly and his group The Crickets – "Rave On", "Tell Me How" and "I'm Looking For Someone To Love".

With production duties handed over to Ron Richards, who also produced the successful Hollies, The Paramounts re-recorded "Poison Ivy" on 1 November 1963 along with "I Feel Good All Over". Both were covers of American rhythm 'n' blues songs, "Poison Ivy" being a Leiber & Stoller-penned hit for The Coasters. The Paramounts performed the song on television in connection with its release on 6 December, and it became a minor hit.

Only a few months earlier the group had played a gig with the Rolling Stones and discovered to their great surprise that there was another UK band performing the same kind of material as themselves. Gary Brooker:

"Our manager ran a gig down in Deal in Kent and this particular night he had The Rolling Stones on with us at the dance hall down there. In fact that week The Stones had 'Come On' out as a single [June 1963]. Kent, Suffolk, Essex was our area, if you like. At this stage The Rolling Stones weren't known outside their circle, which was Reading, Guildford, Maidenhead, Windsor, a bit of West London around Richmond where they would sell out any dance floor they played in.

"Anyway, this gig in Deal was the first time we'd seen The Stones, and they saw us. In fact, we all ended up hiding in the same room, because there was a terrible fight. The Marines had to be 'taught a lesson'. Our manager, who ran the dance hall, brought down these 'heavies' from the Krays' snooker hall, and it was a pretty fearsome battle. Our side, if you like, were wandering around looking for somebody to kill with baseball bats and chains in their hands. I can remember looking out of the window with Mick Jagger and we saw one of these Marines run into his car and lock the door and one of our boys just went up, punched the window, which smashed immediately, and grabbed him by the ears and pulled him out and kicked the hell out of him. A vicious, brutal fight. We were all in the same boat there. We became quite close within the space of a half hour because we were all scared together!"[5]

The fact that The Rolling Stones also debuted as a recording group in 1963 puts into focus the similarities between these two pioneering bands. Furthermore, the Stones for their second release chose to record their own version of "Poison Ivy". However, the single was withdrawn in the UK, possibly to avoid a collision with The Paramounts' release on EMI. Instead it was included on The Rolling Stones' first EP, from January 1964.

Playing the records back to back, the two performances come across as entirely different. While The Paramounts' version is tight and energetic, The Rolling Stones' "Poison Ivy" is of course charmingly shambolic.

The Paramounts' first single very much signalled what lay ahead for them on the recording front. Nearly all their releases are typical of the musical style which in some circles at the time was termed rhythm 'n' blues. However, this is a difficult genre to pin down, particularly since the British and the Americans have different definitions of it.

If we talk specifically of British rhythm 'n' blues it is in reality a unique way to approach playing blues-based pop songs with a rock 'n' roll beat, simple structures (though surprisingly seldom a traditional twelve-bar blues structure), and arrangements based on rather strictly played riffs and melodic patterns.

The song structure found on "Poison Ivy" is typical: verse/chorus – verse/chorus – bridge – verse/chorus – fade riff. Similar simple structures can be found later on in most Procol Harum songs (often with the bridge substituted by a guitar or organ solo), supporting the argument that despite the group's reputation for having invented Progressive Rock with its unorthodox and elaborate structuring they nevertheless kept one foot solidly planted in basic popular music.

The riff on "Poison Ivy" is taken from the original version by The Coasters but emphasised by letting bass, guitar, and to a certain extent piano perform it in unison. On the chorus Brooker plays the kind of traditional rock 'n' roll eight-to-the-bar right hand chord style he would later utilise on Procol Harum songs such as "Conquistador" and "Shine On Brightly".

The B-side, "I Feel Good All Over", is built around a distinctive piano riff repeated over different bass notes as the song moves along, again a technique used on several Procol Harum tracks, perhaps most notably "Quite Rightly So" from 1968 (where Matthew Fisher's organ plays the riff). Likewise Robin Trower's staccato rhythm playing is a forerunner for what he would later be doing in the early days of Procol Harum.

As with "Poison Ivy", and nearly all subsequent Paramounts recordings, Gary Brooker's voice on "I Feel Good All Over" is double-tracked, partly singing a harmony below the lead voice, partly in unison. There is a fine little piano solo displaying his deep admiration for Ray Charles but, as on practically all the group's EMI recordings, a lot of subtle details are drowned by excessive use of reverb and compression. John Denton:

"Around the time when The Paramounts' debut single was recorded Bo Diddley visited Southend. All the group members attended the show and were wildly impressed. What happened next was typical for their enthusiasm and energy. Before this show there had been no Bo Diddley songs in the group's repertoire, but within a few days they had already incorporated a whole handful of them into their set. An even bigger event occurred the following year when Ray Charles played the local Odeon. Again The Paramounts attended."

1964 would become the band's most active year by far at EMI's famous Abbey Road Studios. It started on 15 January when they recorded both "Bad Blood" (another Leiber & Stoller song) and "Chills And Fever".

"Bad Blood", with its high energy-level and slightly unusual structure, is perhaps the best A-side The Paramounts ever released. "Chills And Fever" (which didn't see the light of day until the release of the 1998 EMI CD, *The Paramounts At Abbey Road*) is much more indicative of how the band sounded "live" than anything released during their lifetime. It features a blistering mixture of solo and rhythm guitar typical of the style which many lead guitarists would play at the time, but few mastered to this degree.

"Little Bitty Pretty One", recorded later the same month, is basically a one-chord riff driven along by hand claps and some dynamic bass playing by Diz Derrick. Recorded on the same day was "A Certain Girl", a tongue-in-cheek duet between Brooker and Trower which unfortunately doesn't quite reach the heights of the Yardbirds' version from the same year. The two sides were released on 28 February.

Around the same time a single by fellow-Southender Duffy Power saw the light of day featuring The Paramounts as a backing group.

"Parchman Farm"/"Tired Broke And Busted" is indeed a very nice slice of 1964 British rhythm 'n' blues. With its natural, basic production it could be argued that this record captures the real impact of The Paramounts better than any of their own releases at the time, save for the fact that Duffy Power is responsible for the lead vocals.

Likewise "Stupidity", recorded in 1964 but not released until 1998, comes close to the rawness of the "real" group. The guitar is louder than normal and Trower performs an excellent solo, while there are some exciting things going on in the bass department.

In April the group recorded "It Won't Be Long", the first-ever song written by Brooker and Trower. It was Ron Richards who suggested the band write their own material.

Brooker told me that the song was "written faster than it was recorded". Nevertheless, the track is more structurally advanced and quite simply includes more chord changes than was normal in The Paramounts' repertoire, suggesting what lay ahead a few years further down the line.

"Pride And Joy", a Marvin Gaye composition and not exactly the band's most convincing performance, was recorded in October along with the even less impressive "Do I", featuring some rather peculiar and corny singing from Gary Brooker. "Do I" ended up on the B-side of "Bad Blood", which had been stuck on the shelf since January, suggesting that Parlophone originally had intended to make "Pride And Joy" the A-side but owing to lack of success with the recording went for an older and previously abandoned track instead ("Pride And Joy" is yet another song that remained unreleased until 1998).

None of The Paramounts singles apart from "Poison Ivy" did anything commercially, but "Bad Blood" sold particularly poorly as it got banned by the BBC. Unbeknown to the group, who had performed the song "live" for ages, it was claimed that the title was slang for syphilis.

The recording of "Pride And Joy" signalled The Paramounts' moving into a more soul inspired territory. The reason for this was that Gary Brooker had become friendly with the now legendary Guy Stevens, who worked as a disc jockey at the famous Crawdaddy Club. Guy Stevens soon took over from Tony Wilkinson as The Paramounts' main supplier of cover material and later became an important influence on the early career of Procol Harum.

"I'm The One Who Loves You", a Curtis Mayfield composition, is another indication of this new direction. It also featured Brooker moving from acoustic to electric piano. Trying to tackle a Curtis Mayfield song can't have been any less frightening than recording "Poison Ivy". Mayfield at the time was a member of the vocal trio The Impressions. They had a raw, masculine maturity that a group of English teenagers could never match. However, as with the Beat Boom in general it is exactly the boyish optimism-against-all-odds that wins you over, as energy and charm replace the experience and vibrancy of the original.

Playing The Paramounts' version of "I'm The One Who Loves You" back to back with the original provides a good example of what happened when young British bands in the mid-sixties tackled this kind of material. The Impressions' performance is slow and dynamic, the vocals are mainly sung in falsetto, and the understated beat is provided by the drummer using brushes instead of sticks. Furthermore, a varied colouration of the overall sound is provided by the inclusion of electric organ and trombone.

The Paramounts' version of the same song is considerably faster and based on a more straightforward beat. The performance is entirely self-contained with no use of outside musicians nor any straying away from the basic instrumentation. All in all it is a more "live", more tightly executed and – it has to be said – less soulful rendition than The Impressions' own version. The main similarity is in the quality of the musicianship, which is expert in both cases, but otherwise the recordings are so dissimilar in approach that it almost becomes irrelevant that they are based on the same song.

"I'm The One Who Loves You" was released on 10 July 1964 with "It Won't Be Long" on the flip. A few months later BJ Wilson temporarily left The Paramounts. As Kenny White explains, "I was with a group called Jimmy Powell's Five Dimensions and I asked Barrie to join us and he did. It was a short-lived band."[6] This group also included guitarist Martin Shaw and had previously been a backing band for Rod Stewart.

BJ Wilson's position in The Paramounts was briefly taken over by Phil Wainman (later a successful record producer). Wainman was a more out-going player than Wilson, and his drumming extremely energetic. He played on "You've Got What I Want" and "Turn On

Your Lovelight", all recorded at Abbey Road in November 1964. These tracks have some strong potential and certainly possess their moments of brilliance, but they generally suffer from what appears to be Wainman's ambition to become Britain's answer to Sandy Nelson. They were never released at the time but appear both on the Edsel album and *At Abbey Road* which also contains a fourth Wainman track "Hey Little Girl". The group also did some gigs around this time with Phil Wainman, as Diane Rolph (long-standing fan and editor of fanzine *Shine On*) describes:

"It wasn't the same. We went to see Barrie play with his new band. He admitted that he wasn't happy but didn't want to admit it to The Paramounts. A phone call to Gary ensured that Barrie's feelings were known, and much to our delight he was back in his drumseat at the next gig."[7]

Shortly after Wilson's return the band recorded "Blue Ribbons" and "Cuttin' In". Both songs were overdubbed with orchestral arrangements and released as a single on 23 April 1965 (the non-overdubbed version of "Blue Ribbons" is also included on *At Abbey Road*). The group played "Blue Ribbons" on *Ready Steady Go* followed by a rendition of James Brown's "Darling Little Thing".

The single is an interesting release, being the first time Gary Brooker's voice can be heard with an orchestra. Of the two tracks "Blue Ribbons" is by far the less impressive. Luckily, "Cuttin' In" is an infinitely better performance. Written by legendary bluesman Johnny "Guitar" Watson, it is an almost note-for-note rendition of the original, which finally gives Robin Trower the opportunity to play in a style only very few guitarists in Britain at the time were capable of mastering. Listening to this recording it is hard to believe that the guitar player is a white nineteen year-old boy from Southend.

The fact that EMI went for the considerably weaker but poppier "Blue Ribbons" when choosing the A-side for the single puts us at the centre of the problem here. When seen in isolation The Paramounts' records are a handful of generally interesting and sometimes splendid mid-sixties beat group releases. However, viewed in the light of later endeavours and the unique qualities the band to all accounts possessed in a "live" situation, they become a much less uplifting testament to a truly fantastic combo whose talents got squeezed between demands from the outside world.

Furthermore, there are a number of other explanations why the band didn't have more commercial success. One is that practically no other groups with a line-up similar to theirs made it big in the mid-sixties. The idea of centering a group on a singer-pianist was at this point seen as old-fashioned, something that jazz groups did or, in the best of cases, people like Ray Charles and Jerry Lee Lewis, who had emerged from the first rhythm 'n' blues wave in the 1950s. During the early to mid-sixties British "R&B explosion", guitar bands were in vogue, and if groups included keyboards – which an increasing number of them did after The Animals' big hit in 1964 with "House Of The Rising Sun" – it would nearly always be electric organs.

Gary Brooker might at times have considered shifting to a Vox or Farfisa organ (Hammonds for financial reasons being beyond the reach of most young groups), which would have suited The Paramounts' repertoire. What kept him from doing so was probably the fact that he was a true pianist with a style that was practically impossible to adapt to organ. He arguably wouldn't have been comfortable playing a Vox, which he may not even have liked the sound of. Instead he bought himself a Hohner Clavinette, a small electric piano which was also much easier to amplify and carry around on the road than a real piano.

Another disadvantage the group suffered from was that they really weren't very good at doing vocal harmonies. These were provided mainly by Trower and Derrick, both capable singers but not particularly good backing vocalists.

This was a weakness The Paramounts shared with many British groups at the time, but in their case it became particularly problematic around mid-1964 when they started moving into soul territory, a style often dominated by superb vocal harmony work. On a few occasions Ron Richards called upon the services of The Breakaways to assist on Paramounts recordings. They were an experienced and much-used trio of girl singers often employed for sessions at the time, but very "white" and English-sounding.

Perhaps it would have been a better idea if Richards had involved a couple of the guys from The Hollies instead, just for studio recordings. Such a combination could have been extremely interesting but would of course have meant a further investment for EMI.

However, it could also be argued that The Paramounts' problem quite simply was that they were too young and their talents weren't yet developed enough for them to become a major success. As Robin Trower put it to me, "The Paramounts weren't really a serious band. They were just mucking about."

This statement is supported by Brooker's remark that the band would probably have preferred not to make records at all. They were a small, constantly-touring R&B combo of teenage guys playing covers of American records, and so far they really had no ambitions to make it any further than that.

This also explains why they didn't write more of their own material, though their two attempts during 1964/65, both relegated to B-sides, weren't at all bad .

In particular "Don't Ya Like My Love" from June/July 1965 is a fine song and a much better performance than their bland attempt at the same time to record Van McCoy's "Baby I'm Yours" and Payne Carroll's "Draw Me Closer" (both featuring backing vocals by The Breakaways). "Draw Me Closer" ended up on an obscure French EP, while "Baby I'm Yours" for good reasons went straight into the vaults, and "Don't You Like My Kind Of Love" became the flip of the dire "You Never Had It So Good".

Roadrunners

"Much to the concern of our mothers we started travelling long distances to see them ... a gruelling tour of one-nighters, Manchester one night, Weybridge the next, with a return trip to Southend in between. Diz did the driving, Kellogs and Cobbles roadied."

Diane Rolph[8]

No one seems to remember exactly when the Shades Club closed, but it appears to have coincided with The Paramounts' leaving Southend for a while to gig in other corners of the country. As John "Kellogs" Kalinowski remembers:

"A typical gig with The Paramounts around that time would start with everyone being picked up by Diz. That was quite a task in itself, particularly during the time when Barrie had moved back to Ponders End in North London. We'd normally stop by at his place to eat some white bread fried egg sandwiches. That was BJ's big thing. Then we'd probably head off for Manchester, where the band had a particularly enthusiastic following.

"The driving was a real pain in the neck – at least eight hours in the back of this little van. In those days they were only just building Britain's motorway network, so there would always be roadworks. We'd be stuck in queues for hours and it would be either freezing cold or boiling hot as I recall it. No wonder we all got heavily into reading. I particularly remember Robin being a big science fiction fan.

"Sometimes we'd stay up there for a few days. The band would be sleeping at various bed & breakfasts, while I'd be sleeping out in the van. Guarding the equipment, they called it. That was their excuse. I was very much the low man, but I enjoyed it, there was an amazing ambience around these guys. They were talented, they had a good sense of humour. I was a couple of years younger than them, so I was eager to serve. They paid me one pound a week each. I was living on a staple diet of Mars bars."

When The Paramounts returned to play the Studio Jazz Club in Southend in 1965 local fans found that they had become "a different group", as John Denton recalls:

"The old upright piano in the Shades Club had been a strong feature in the past. Now things were different. The Hohner Clavinette, which Gary had acquired in the meantime, had a mellower sound and fewer keys, meaning that a lot of the rock 'n' roll attitudes automatically had to go, and the same went for the Ray Charles songs."

Furthermore the group's image had been "straightened up", at least for photo sessions and the like, in the sense that the members now appeared in neat haircuts, uniform suede waistcoats and blue suede boots on such occasions.

Nevertheless, by this time The Paramounts' career was gradually beginning to go sour as they were increasingly forced to make their living by backing other artists such as Sandie Shaw. They appeared on stage with Shaw for three weeks at the Olympia in Paris, and also toured other parts of Continental Europe both on their own and as a backing band for solo artists. These activities partly came via the group's signing up with Brian Epstein's management company, NEMS.

EMI were presumably getting tired of seeing their investment in the group go down the drain. The Paramounts on the other hand felt that their record company had never really understood what they were all about. On their last single, "You Never Had It So Good", Gary Brooker sang in a deliberately atrocious way as a protest against being told to release a song which was far removed from the style of music The Paramounts were truly keen on playing. Some encouragement did come via NEMS and an offer to play support for The Beatles during their last tour of Britain in December 1965.

"It was a package tour of England," John Kalinowski told me. "I particularly remember when they played the Finsbury Park Astoria in London, the venue that later became The Rainbow. The first set always ended with a top name in those days, and on this occasion it was The Moody Blues. The Paramounts opened the second set. They were backing singers Steve Aldo and Beryl Marsden, and perhaps they did a couple of their own songs too."

"I used to stand out in the wings and watch The Beatles", Gary Brooker recalled. "Out in front of the stage it was mayhem, of course. But I could see them and hear them quite well from where I stood, so I reckon I'm one of the few people who have really heard The Beatles playing 'live'.

"We got along fine with them, but you couldn't really socialise with The Beatles. I mean, they couldn't go to a restaurant or the cinema or anything like that.

"I recall a sound check where BJ hadn't shown up for some reason and Paul McCartney sat in on drums for us, but generally George Harrison was the easiest one to get along with. He'd always be more generous to pass his joint around."

Brooker's relationship with The Beatles' members, particularly George Harrison and Ringo Starr, would continue in years to come. However, by the spring of 1966 The Paramounts were a severely disillusioned band. They carried on through the early months of the year, while the scene around them was changing and British rhythm 'n' blues and pop was turning into psychedelia.

It would be wrong to say that this new environment left no room for an interest in soul and R&B; but the interest that existed was more and more turning towards the original American artists.

"As we were getting into 1966," Brooker recalled, "things like Sam & Dave, Otis Redding, and that sort of R&B was becoming popular in its own right. So where we could originally pick our songs and be the only people doing them, suddenly people were listening to the actual originals down the discotheque. We sort of lost the excitement, lost the enjoyment of it."

"At one of the very last gigs they did, a club somewhere south of London", John Kalinowski remembers, "this guy turned up whom I'd never seen before. Someone said his name was Keith Reid and that he was supposed to write songs with Gary. Shortly after the group went on tour in Germany with Chris Andrews. I didn't go with them, I stayed in Southend and worked in a bakery for some months until 'A Whiter Shade Of Pale' had become a hit and I joined Gary again as a roadie for Procol Harum."

Robin Trower in fact left The Paramounts before the group actually stopped playing. This coincided with the offer to go on tour with pop singer Chris Andrews.

"We'd already backed Sandie Shaw off and on for a year and Rob certainly didn't like that," Gary Brooker said. "To us it was just a way of making some money, but he didn't like it. And when the Chris Andrews gig came along – that was the last straw for Rob. He said, 'I'm not doing it.' We said, 'Okay, we'll just do it and then we'll probably pack up.'"

Robin Trower was replaced by the late Martin Shaw, who had been in Jimmy Powell's Five Dimensions two year earlier with BJ Wilson, and furthermore the line-up was augmented with a sax player for this last tour.

Before finally throwing in the towel in the early autumn of 1966, The Paramounts made one last recording. It was to be their finest hour. On 20 June 1966, when Trower was still in the band, they entered Abbey Road Studios with a dozen of their friends and recorded "Freedom", a song written by jazz legend Charlie Mingus. Like all the other recordings the group had made over the three preceding years it was a strict three-hour session, but generally the sprit was looser than ever before.

"'Freedom' wasn't like anything we'd done, and probably sums up the sort of influences that were in the air round about the time we stopped playing", Gary Brooker remembered. "I myself became interested in jazz. I'd never liked jazz at all, but I heard two people one night around somebody's place. I heard Art Blakey and I heard Charlie Mingus and it changed me world at the time."

Recorded less than ten months before "A Whiter Shade Of Pale", "Freedom" is the one song that most clearly links The Paramounts with Procol Harum. It has some fine guitar licks, an organ solo, a blues guitar solo, and recited lyrics. Even the instrumental bridge, built over a repeated ascending bass line, has similarities with a certain passage featured on Harum's 1970 masterpiece, "Whaling

Stories". Incidentally, the recording also drew upon a minor crowd of invited friends for backing vocals.

"Freedom" wasn't released until 1983, so the link is visible only from a retrospective point of view. Nevertheless, the song signals the end of an era, of years of running up and down the British mainland and sometimes across to the Continent, four teenage musicians, their roadie and their instruments and equipment squeezed together in a small van with the words *Paramounts R&B* painted in gold letters on the back.

Luckily, it also signals a new beginning with even better things to come.

Part Two

"A pretty weird bunch", 1966-1967

Sock it to me, Josef K.

Still living inside us are the dark, secret corridors, blind windows, dirty yards, noisy pubs and secluded hotels ... The unhealthy old Jewish quarter inside us is much more real than the hygienic new town around us ... Awakening we walk through a dream: no more than ghosts of forgotten times.

Franz Kafka

Recipe for success. Take one unemployed lyric-writer and couple him with a disillusioned ex-member of a commercially unsuccessful rhythm 'n' blues group. Add a drop-out music student who recently persuaded his grandmother to lend him some money to buy a Hammond organ yet hasn't quite decided if he wants to be Jimmy Smith or Johann Sebastian Bach.

Then add a dead solid and simple bass player, a guitarist with a Bob Dylan haircut, and a studio drummer called in for the day.

The result? A Number 1 all-time world-wide hit!

Of course it wasn't quite that simple. These stories always have a middle man, a go-between. In this case it was Guy Stevens, the music guru and disc jockey who had become a friend of Gary Brooker during 1964. Stevens was an associate of Chris Blackwell, the director of Island Records. Island had formerly been a label mainly for ska music. However, around 1966 the company was expanding its musical scope by signing bands in a new evolving musical style, soon known as psychedelia.

One day a young man managed to get a meeting with Blackwell in his office. The visitor had been listening to a lot of Bob Dylan and, as he would put it himself many years later, "could see how to do it". What he meant was that he had discovered he could write good song lyrics. The young man's name was Keith Reid.

Keith Brian Stuart Reid was born on 10 October 1946 and grew up in London's East End, more precisely Mile End Road, then an important part of the city's Jewish district.

In the 1940s the Jewish population in the area consisted mainly of second- or third-generation immigrants whose forefathers had arrived in England as a consequence of the pogroms in Russia and Poland in the 1880s and 1890s. These people were traditionally working-class and had assimilated pretty well, while still retaining some of their cultural distinctiveness. They would often work in the "rag trade"; some of them were tailors, others ran little shops and workshops in the area.

Another considerably smaller group of immigrants had arrived by the end of the 1930s, mainly intellectuals who had been chased out of Germany and Austria by the Nazis. Robbed of all their savings and belongings they managed to escape to England. They too would often settle in London's East End, penniless and with nothing to resemble their former high society status.

Britain had its Nazis too, led by the notorious Oswald Moseley. There were demonstrations and violent confrontations in London's East End between the Black-shirts and the local Jewish community. After that came the Second World War. The Blitz hit the East End particularly hard and many families had to move out into the countryside.

Some evacuated Londoners didn't return to the capital until a long while after the War had ended. The city was so badly bombed that for many there simply wasn't anything to return home to. In the Mile End Road practically every third house had been razed to the ground by the Luftwaffe. Long into the 1950s bomb-sites surrounded by billboards were still a strong feature in the townscape.

This was the world Keith Reid grew up in.

"I was born in a place called Welwyn Garden City," he told me. "That was where my mother was evacuated to during the War because of the bombing. So I was only born there, I didn't live there. I always lived in London."

The family moved back to a house in Mile End Road. When I asked Reid if he received a very Orthodox, Jewish upbringing, he replied, "No, absolutely not. I've always rejected religion."

Though Reid in recent years has started to open up much more, in interviews he still tends to be evasive about two subjects in particular – the meaning behind his lyrics, and details about his private life including his upbringing. However, one thing he has often emphasised is that his social background is working-class.

Since Keith Reid doesn't have a hint of a working-class accent and at least in some ways appears to be an intellectual, this mention of working-class roots has puzzled many. The explanation seems to be that the working-class element is only there in a strict sociological sense. Culturally and mentally the Jewish community – particularly those who had escaped from the Nazis in mainland Europe (the group that Reid's parents allegedly belonged to) – would be quite different from the rest of the East End and British working-class people in general.

That also solves the mystery of why Keith Reid, in a surprisingly revealing interview with Paul Carter in Procol Harum fanzine *Shine On* (July 1997), mentions being under heavy pressure from both his parents and his brother and sister to carry on in school after obligatory training. He didn't take their advice. In fact he left school when he was fifteen. Reid told Paul Carter that it was partly a rebellion against the pressures his academically inclined family put on him, partly a reaction to feeling uncomfortable at school and quite simply loathing the concept of "being taught". Instead, Reid describes himself around this time as a bit of a self-educator:

"My mother taught me to read at a very early age, when I was about four or so, and I read constantly and voraciously until I left school when I was 15. And my background for writing songs, I always think a lot of it came from all the reading I did. I read so much. I'd just go to Mile End Library, my parents let me use their tickets as well so I used to go not just into the children's library but upstairs into the grown-ups' library as well, and I just used to get seven or eight books and take them home, read them and go back ... I just used to grab anything off the shelf that looked interesting. It was my escape, really. I escaped into a world of books."[9]

During the post-war period the Jewish district in the East End still retained a certain air of the old Eastern Europe. How important this and in fact the whole Jewish element is to an understanding of Keith Reid's work is practically anyone's guess, but it doesn't take much of an effort to find significant parallels between him and the famous Jewish writer Franz Kafka (who lived all his life in Prague).

There are, particularly in Reid's early lyrics, a number of features which are noticeably Kafka-esque – a deep dissatisfaction with one-self, with mundane daily life, and with common people (the crowd); a profound feeling of undefined guilt, of having committed some momentous sin which apparently doesn't even have a name, of para-noia and claustrophobia. Finally, both writers make elaborate use of grotesque imagery, emotional extremes, and a sometimes-relieving sense of humour.

Perhaps more than being specifically Jewish these feelings could also be summed up as "the white man's blues", which immediately brings us right to the core of Procol Harum. It brings us to the very place where – artistically – Keith Reid met Gary Brooker.

Through the 1950s the Jewish community in London's East End dwindled fast as the younger generation started to get education and better jobs. In thousands they left the area with its appallingly poor housing in order to find better places to live and raise their families.

Perhaps as a defence against increasing pressures from the sur-roundings, young boys belonging to the remaining Jewish families in the area started forming exclusive little "gangs" establishing their own ethos. They would be well-dressed, neat, isolated and sectarian, seem-ingly using arrogance as a means of self-protection. In an attempt to shake off a historic burden that was too much to bear they would emphasize an ideal of "living for the moment" and be "modern" in every sense of the word – dress, thinking, musical tastes. Keith Reid belonged to this new movement and so did Marc Feld, later known as Marc Bolan.

"Long before the Mod movement," Keith Reid told *Mojo*'s Rob Chapman (12.3.97), "when they were still being referred to as Modernists – there were two teams, one in the East End, one in the Stamford Hill area, which was where Marc lived. Everybody used to go and hang out at a Wimpy Bar near Whitechapel Art Gallery on a Sunday morning. I was 12 and I thought I was the youngest kid on the scene, but he was even younger. First time I met him he was very proudly wearing a pair of Levi's which he'd pinched from this shop in Leman Street. We just got talking 'cause we were the youngest in this scene of people who totally lived for clothes. We were two precocious snot-nosed kids. Then I didn't see him for years, until I read a piece by Maureen Cleave in the *Evening Standard* about this kid Marc Bolan who had made a record called 'The Wizard'. He performed it on *Ready Steady Go!*, but it didn't do anything. His mother used to have a fruit stall in Wardour Street and Marc was still helping out on Saturdays. Neither of us were working and we were both writing lyrics, so we got pally again. Then I got together with Gary and the next thing I knew I had a hit record. Marc started Tyrannosaurus Rex and we both ended up on the same record label."

The early relationship between the two boys apparently went a little deeper than indicated by Reid in this interview. In 1972 Bolan's parents told *Record Mirror* about their son, "He used to sit and write songs with Keith Reid, who went on to be part of Procol Harum. They were mates. They'd just sit together and write music from morning till night in our house. That's all they'd ever talk about – music. That and how they'd get on and what they'd do when they were well-known."

Earlier on Keith Reid had shown an interest in playing music. He had classical piano lessons as a child and even won a Junior Exhibitor Scholarship to Trinity College of Music. However, at the age of twelve he gave up playing.

"I lost interest in it," he told me. "Then I got into writing when I was about eighteen. To write, I suppose Bob Dylan inspired me. But I was always into music – rock 'n' roll and rhythm 'n' blues... I had lots of different jobs. Just odd jobs. I think I was unemployed when I met Gary."

Not knowing anybody in the music business Keith Reid started taking his lyrics around to all the companies. As already mentioned, one of the people he went to see was Chris Blackwell at Island Records, whom he offered the publishing rights to his songs. But there was a catch; Reid wanted to go to New York and become famous. Blackwell could have the publishing rights to his lyrics but only on the condition that he advanced him the money to go to the USA.

Chris Blackwell was somewhat unimpressed and shoved Keith Reid in the direction of one of his A&R men, who seemed to have a soft spot for unusual artists. This employee was Guy Stevens. Steve Hyams – the guitarist-singer-songwriter who joined Mott The Hoople in the later stages of their career – vividly remembers Guy Stevens around this time:

"Guy was a friend of Brian Jones and constantly looking for some new act that had the same quality as The Stones. He was mad about them, and mad about Jerry Lee Lewis, and mad about Bob Dylan. He was a total speed freak too, traces of white powder all over his flat. But he had an incredible way of looking at things and coming up with group names, one-liners. He suggested the names for people such as Spooky Tooth and Mott The Hoople. So he was crazy and also a genius in his own kind of way."

Guy Stevens was impressed enough with Keith Reid's lyrical efforts to try teaming him up with Stevie Winwood. Winwood, still in his teens but already becoming an institution in British rock, was then a member of the highly successful Fontana-signed Spencer Davis Group. However, he had plans to break away from this group and start Traffic, a more psychedelia-inspired outfit. Reid went to meet Stevie Winwood but found that he was too involved in working with Jim Capaldi, who arguably thought it unnecessary to let an outside lyric writer into the camp.

The next person Stevens tried teaming Keith Reid up with was Pete Townshend of The Who. Quite content with writing his own lyrics Townshend mentioned Reid to the members of Cream, who were looking for a writer. Eventually they chose to work with Pete Brown instead, and Keith Reid once again found himself getting nowhere.

"Musicians wanted for Dylan-type band"

Procol Harum was a brainchild of Keith Reid.

Matthew Fisher

"One afternoon I was over at Guy's place and Keith was there and we were introduced to each other", Gary Brooker recalled. "Guy said to me, 'Keith writes words – lyrics. Why don't you put some music to them?' What made Guy think of that, I don't know, because I had never written any music... Anyway, I went home with this envelope full of words from Keith. I think I read them but didn't do anything about them for a while."

At this point The Paramounts were still going. Keith Reid went to see them perform, the initial idea being that he should provide them with lyrics so that Gary Brooker could write his own songs for the group.

"I hadn't heard about them before," Keith Reid told me. "I hadn't really been involved with the music scene before then. I was trying to get into it... I didn't hear from Gary for a very long time. Whether it was as much as a year, I can't remember ... "

Various factors indicate that it couldn't possibly have been more than a few months. But the fact of the matter is that Keith Reid eventually became impatient with not hearing anything from Gary Brooker and wrote him a letter to learn how things were developing.

"The first envelope Keith had given me had about ten lyrics in it," Brooker said. "But it wasn't until a few months later that I got them out again. I put them on the piano, and suddenly I had written about three songs. I was quite amazed with myself. I enjoyed it."

When I first interviewed Gary Brooker, some sixteen years after the event, the excitement of that experience was still present as an undertone in his voice. Here he was, sitting on a normal day at the piano in his mother's house – a young, white English pianist and singer with a rudimentary knowledge of classical music but primarily in love with black American rhythm 'n' blues. The problem was that by now life had taught him that unless he found something to do with this music other than just copy the original artists, he would get nowhere. Looking at Reid's lyrics it must suddenly have started to dawn on him that here was a whole new direction to go in.

These songs incorporated the aforementioned feeling of "white man's blues", and the structures were much the same as in straightforward pop songs. What Gary Brooker did with these lyrics was in one sense extremely logical. He instinctively translated them into a musical style. The blues, the pop, the anachronistic element – all these ingredients were reflected in Brooker's music right from the start.

"One of the first songs I wrote was 'Something Following Me'", he told me. "I was thinking of making a Ray Charlesy kind of song for that one. By coincidence, the next day I got this letter from Keith – this is a few months after I first met him – and he just put, 'Dear Gary...' and he quoted some of the lines from 'Something Following Me' and wrote, 'Any luck with the words, please get in touch.' I thought, 'That's great.' So I went down to the phone box straight away. I said, 'Keith! It's funny, I've just written a couple of songs.' So he came down and he liked them and so we started working on the other ones."

During the following months Keith Reid and Gary Brooker would sit together at the piano a couple of days every week and write various songs. Reid wasn't really part of the making of the music, but Brooker would play him a few sequences and he would either agree to them or not. Gary Brooker:

"He came down one day and said, 'I just thought of a word on the train – *Conquistador!*' I said, 'Well, fine, what is it?' He said, 'Some sort of Spanish cavalier.' So he wrote the words and I wrote the

48

music. We went on like that for a couple of months until we had about ten or twelve songs written."

Luckily for Brooker and Reid, what they had embarked upon went hand in hand with some changes that were in the air at the time. After the release of The Beatles' *Rubber Soul* and *Revolver* albums, not to mention The Beach Boys' *Pet Sounds*, the rock music scene had started to move towards something much more stylistically adventurous than beat combos pouring out two minute singles.

Ever at the forefront of musical development, The Beatles had already been flirting with classical influences, but they were really able to do so only by drawing on the talents of their producer George Martin, who for instance wrote and played the Bach-inspired piano solo on "In My Life". Likewise in California, The Byrds' guitarist Roger McGuinn had started to incorporate Bach themes into his own unique folk/rock idiom, while another US group called The Left Banke enjoyed considerable success during 1966 with their single "Walk Away Renee". Built over a descending bass line, this song had some strong classical undertones and even a string arrangement written by group member Mike Brown. This was something very new to the world at the time. Though Brooker denies being consciously inspired by Mike Brown's band he gladly admits to "being aware of them and what they were doing".

To cut a long story short, throughout 1966 something was brewing underneath the surface of British pop which Brooker and Reid could easily associate themselves with. It probably wasn't a conscious move on their behalf, it was just that times were changing and people with minds and backgrounds like theirs were starting to have their day.

The only problem was that by now The Paramounts had split up and Gary Brooker had no intention of ever playing in a group again. The last year in particular had been a deep disappointment to him, so at the age of just 21 he had decided to retire from playing in groups. Instead the initial plan was for him and Keith Reid to become non-performing songwriters.

Consequently, the two of them started approaching people in the music business with the intention of selling their songs to other artists, only to find that the timing for a venture of this nature was somewhat misplaced. By late 1966 most British groups preferred to write their own material rather than put their faith in outside songwriters.

This was partly because of a trend set by The Beatles, partly because it had started to dawn on musicians that the real earnings in popular music are not in performing as much as in writing. The people who still didn't write their own material were mainly performers leaning towards entertainment or easy listening material. Arguably, Brooker and Reid's failure in selling themselves as a songwriting team was caused by their material being much too innovative and unusual for these kinds of artists.

"We started going to a few of my old contacts," said Brooker. "I remember we went to see Andrew Loog Oldham and he put us in a studio."

Two attempts were made at this early stage to record the songs Brooker and Reid had written so far. One featured a group consisting of Gary Brooker himself, BJ Wilson, guitarist Kenny White and a now-forgotten bass player (White until recently remembered him as Alan Cartwright, who much later joined Procol Harum – but Cartwright denies having played on this session). According to Kenny White the result was truly awful, which may be why another session was recorded by Brooker alone, just singing and playing piano. Apparently, none of these recordings exist today. It seems that only the tapes featuring Gary Brooker on his own were used for demonstration purposes. However, he and Keith Reid still didn't have any success in selling their song material.

"We didn't try for very long," said Keith Reid. "It just became obvious that the only thing to do was to form a group." So one day during a meeting at Guy Stevens' place Reid turned to Brooker and suggested he get a new band together to perform the songs himself.

"I was pushing it along," Keith Reid recalled, "because I had never experienced any setbacks, so I probably had the enthusiasm. I didn't see how it could fail. I didn't have any doubt in my mind, I thought our first record was gonna be a big hit – be as big as The Beatles."

Eventually Brooker gave in and the two of them asked Guy Stevens if he could come up with a name for the new group they were about to form. He suggested they name themselves after a Burmese cat belonging to a friend of his.

Soon afterwards an advert appeared in the *Melody Maker* searching for musicians to form a band by the name of Procol Harum.

Hazy days

The music was fantastic, it had all these unusual descending chord progressions – in fact, that ought to have made me realise right from the start which way it was all heading...

Richard Brown (Procol Harum's first guitarist)

Befittingly – considering Procol Harum's Gothic image in their early days – one of the first two musicians to join the group was bassist Dave Knights, soon known to insiders as *The Undertaker*:

"I answered an advert in the back of the *Melody Maker*. It was two guys who wanted to put a band together around their music, their compositions. It was Keith Reid and Gary Brooker. I met them in a flat in Camden Town. They played me some of their music. I thought it was very unusual, very different, very Dylan-orientated and very interesting... They seemed to be impressed with the way I looked. I looked very doomy, all in black and a bit mysterious at that time. Later Keith Reid homed in on that and got me to wear undertaker's jackets!"

Born 28 June 1945, David Knights is a North Londoner from a working-class background. He grew up in Islington, left school at fifteen and worked for four-and-a-half years as a clerk in a solicitor's office.

"I was playing music in my spare time. I started off on guitar. I suppose I was about sixteen. I was the guitarist, and in those days nobody wanted to play bass. It wasn't a very attractive thing to do. Everyone was into Hank Marvin – it was that period. One day during rehearsals another guitarist came along who was a true guitarist, who was very, very good. So the group decision at that time was, okay, become a bass player. I found a bass guitar, a very cheap one, I think the strings were about an inch from the fretboard, and I just listened to records for days and days, every hour of the day, for a couple of months and worked it out and became the bass player of that band... I was very into melody and in my opinion I became a melodic bass player. Maybe not technically wonderful, but melodic."

The intention was for Dave to study to become a solicitor. However, life at the solicitor's office held little excitement for him – "there were cobwebs everywhere and it was very, very stuffy" – so when he was nineteen he started looking through the music papers to find a professional band to play with. Soon afterwards he joined a group called The Establishment.

"A few days after that I got into a van in the Old Kent Road and ended up in Zurich in Switzerland where we played for four or five hours a day, every day, for a couple of months. After that I came back, making a wonderful profit of £9."

After the first meeting in Camden Town, Brooker and Reid invited Dave Knights to an audition. It was to take place on the first floor above a pub called The Roebuck in Tottenham Court Road, and some four or five other bass players turned up to try their luck along with Knights.

Gary Brooker recalled being disappointed on this occasion. "I had arranged with BJ Wilson that he should be there with me at the audition. But he never turned up."

Keith Reid picks up the story, "BJ was gonna be in the group. He was our original choice to be in the group but he kept letting us down because he was with a group that were working and he wasn't prepared to take the plunge and leave them."

However, BJ Wilson wasn't the only one to have doubts about the project. Gary Brooker himself almost went off and joined Dusty Springfield before changing his mind again and putting all his efforts into the group instead.

This situation partly answers the question why Brooker and Reid didn't simply try to reform The Paramounts for their new project. BJ

Wilson was supposed to get involved for a while but eventually decided not to. Diz Derrick had gone back to college to study the flute and take up jazz piano. And Robin Trower never even came into question.

"Rob really wouldn't have wanted to be involved at the start of this," Brooker said. "It would not have interested him. He was definitely excluded from the formula, if you like... He always used to play too loud, he'd always try to drown up the vocals and the piano, and when you're trying to put across some words and a song that's the last thing you want."

At the aforementioned audition, not just bass players but also a number of guitarists had been selected from the interviews and invited. One was Les Lambert, former school friend of BJ Wilson (and later a front-of-house engineer for Procol Harum in the early 1970s).

During a recent conversation I had with Lambert he recalled arriving at The Roebuck at two o'clock in the afternoon with his friend, bassist Tony Jones, and walking up the stairs to the first floor where the audition was to be held.

"It was a long room with windows on one side. People were sitting around in clusters, not saying much to each other. Dave Knights was sitting at the far end by himself – it somehow seemed that he was already chosen for the job as a bass player. Ray Royer immediately caught your eye because of his wild hairstyle. Gary was very quiet and didn't seem too comfortable, but Keith Reid was very much in control of everything."

There was a piano in the room but it wasn't connected to an amplifier of any kind, and Brooker didn't sing during the audition either. Keith Reid paired off guitarists and bass players and tried them out by just encouraging them to "play some blues". Les Lambert:

"Tony and I were taken aback by this, because that was not the type of music we normally played. But we decided to play a Duane Eddy track called 'Three-30-Blues', simply because it had the word 'blues' in it. In fact, we were just about to start when the door opened and this guy stepped in. I immediately thought it was Caleb Quaye, the black guitarist who later played on Elton John's first records. He had some great gear and he looked the part and he glanced around and said, 'Who's Keith?' So Keith said it was him and this guy said, 'You're gonna pay for the cab as we agreed. It's out there waiting.' The rest of us just gasped for air, because he was so self-assured. I mean, this was quite a way to present yourself when you've come looking for a job. Then later when he started playing he just blew the rest of us away.

"I stayed for the rest of the audition and heard all the other candidates. In some cases Gary Brooker would join them on piano, but mostly he wouldn't. He seemed quite reluctant and not at all the same self-assured and talented person I had seen playing with The Paramounts earlier. None of the other guitarists came anywhere near this fellow I mentioned before, so I thought, 'If it's blues they want that's their man.'"

The guitarist with a lot of self-confidence in fact wasn't Caleb Quaye, his name was Richard Brown. Born in 1948 to a Caribbean father and a Scottish mother, he had previously been a member of Birmingham-based The Vogues (whose 1966 single, "Younger Girl", he did *not* play on). As Les Lambert had predicted, Richard Brown was immediately chosen to become Procol Harum's first guitarist.

"At the time when I joined, Procol Harum were supposed to be managed by Guy Stevens," Brown told me. "But as far as I could see he didn't do anything, really." According to Richard Brown, he and Dave Knights were living together for a while in the basement of Guy Stevens' house. It was very damp. They were given camp beds to sleep on and "fed" only once a day.

"Dave and I were literally starving. It was ludicrous, it felt like we were being kept. At that time Procol Harum wasn't at all like a real band. There was no creativity, no camaraderie, no input was allowed from anyone other than Keith and Gary. No vocal harmonies, no guitar solos – in fact I felt they would have preferred it if I'd just been playing acoustic.

"There were long periods where Dave and I were doing nothing, just sitting around in this damp, horrible basement. We tried to pass the time by debating among ourselves who on earth this strange guy Keith Reid was with his little round glasses and French cigarettes. He spoke like he'd been to public school and he and Gary were obviously extremely close. They both lived elsewhere, in fact Gary went home to his mother every time after rehearsals."

The group's rehearsals had to be held in a nearby church hall, since there was no piano at Guy Stevens' place – just thousands of records.

"We were really just like a backing band for Gary," Richard Brown continued. "Which is all right if you get paid for it, but the salary they gave us was so small. When all the expenses had been deducted there wasn't much left at all. And it was all on such an amateurish level. We had this drummer, BJ Wilson, who only had a snare drum, practically. Dave played bass through my amp... But then there was the music and the lyrics, this absolutely unique, astonishing stuff, sung by this fantastic voice, you know. I was amazed that I was actually in a band together with the lead singer of The Paramounts! That was the only reason I was still hanging on, because on all other fronts absolutely nothing was happening."

Richard Brown recalls playing early Brooker-Reid compositions such as "Conquistador", "Homburg", "Cerdes (Outside The Gates Of)", "Pandora's Box", "Salad Days (Are Here Again)", "A Whiter Shade Of Pale" and "Something Following Me" (then referred to as "Tombstone"). Furthermore, he has clear recollections of rehearsing with an organ player who "couldn't make his mind up to join us as he was also with Cat Stevens".

Neither Brown nor anyone else in Procol Harum at this point seems to recall the keyboard player's name. However, investigating a bit further it turns out that Cat Stevens' backing band around this time was George Bean and the Runners, who also backed Lulu on occasions, and on drums featured a certain ex-Paramounts member by the name of BJ Wilson.

Wilson had joined this band shortly after The Paramounts had split up. George Bean himself was a singer and a close friend of Mick Jagger and The Rolling Stones' producer Andrew Loog Oldham, but his own career never really took off. In the autumn of 1966 Tony Catchpole was the lead guitarist in the Runners.

"I remember BJ as a very sophisticated person," he told me. "George and I were already semi-gourmets, but BJ introduced us to Indian food, and I also recall him telling me about smoking opium, which scared the shit out of me. But he was that kind of a guy and obviously very, very talented. I don't actually think the rest of us felt there was much of a chance that he was going to stay with us for very long."

Tony Catchpole recalls that The Runners' Hammond organist at this point was Alan Morris, formerly the group's rhythm guitarist. Persistent attempts to track down this musician have been unsuccessful. George Bean himself died in the early seventies at which time, according to Tony Catchpole, Alan Morris was managing a club near Piccadilly Circus in London. By then he had already stopped being an active musician. However, all indications – including the way he looked and appeared, and the exact instrument he was playing (a Hammond C3, which was pretty rare in those days) – point to Alan Morris being Procol Harum's first organ player.

Sorting out the early history of Procol Harum is an extremely complicated task. Nevertheless I would suggest that sometime in very early 1967 there was a rather unstable line-up consisting of Gary Brooker (vocals, piano), BJ Wilson (drums), David Knights (bass), Richard Brown (guitar), and Alan Morris (Hammond organ). Possibly Wilson and Morris just considered themselves to be "on loan" from George Bean and the Runners. It appears that Wilson didn't even bother to bring along his whole drum kit.

The fact that BJ Wilson was actually in Procol Harum at this early stage may come as a surprise. However, it fits with a statement Gary Brooker made to me that, "BJ was originally part of the group, but he chickened out because there was no money. It was a gamble."

How long this elusive combination of players might have existed for is practically anyone's guess. Probably not much more than two or three weeks. Nevertheless it is an early version of the band which has never before been mentioned in any of the well-known chronicles.

After deciding to leave Procol Harum, Richard Brown went back to his native Birmingham and shortly afterwards moved to Southport where he joined a group called Jasmin T. The light his recollections shed on the earliest stages of the group's history amplifies the general impression of economic and managerial chaos sometimes pointed out in interviews by other group members.

The Miller's Tale

Some guy looked at a chick and said to her, "You've gone a whiter shade of pale." That phrase stuck in my mind. It was a beautiful thing for someone to say. I wish I'd said it.

Keith Reid [10]

It is pretty certain that "A Whiter Shade Of Pale" had been written shortly before the first fragile line-up of Procol Harum came together.

"The songwriting process is a funny one, like making a pot," Reid told Paul Carter (*Shine On*, June 1997). "You get your initial idea. Here I had that line 'A Whiter Shade Of Pale'. So you've got your bit of clay, and then you just try to make a pot out of it. And you use your imagination, you shape it and play with it, until you've got something that looks like a pot, or sounds like a song."

Keith Reid has never claimed to be the original author of the phrase that gave its name to the song. Steve Hyams:

"I went to see Guy Stevens at the time when 'A Whiter Shade Of Pale' had just come out. He was in prison then, the police had arrested him on Brian Jones' roof for drug possession. When I met him he was very upset. He had this newspaper in his hand and he had just found out that the song had gone to Number 1. He claimed that he had come up with that one line 'A Whiter Shade Of Pale' and Reid must have heard him saying it somewhere and built his song around it."

Putting several different stories together you get a version which may be the most accurate one: Keith Reid was at a party where he heard someone use the phrase "A Whiter Shade Of Pale" – he could have been unaware who actually said it, but it seems quite probable that it might have been Guy Stevens.

In Paul Carter's interview Keith Reid speaks quite proudly of his lyric:

"If people can continually debate something, we're talking about thirty years now, it just says to me that it had great depth. If it had been a fairly superficial lyric people would never have got into it."

However, at other times and in different circumstances Reid seems to have expressed the exact opposite feeling. Veteran drummer Mac Poole, who mainly knows Keith Reid from the time when he played in Mickey Jupp's band (who in the late seventies were managed by Reid), told me that, "Keith was just totally dismissive if you even mentioned that song. He said it was nothing, that he had never intended it to be about anything or go anywhere. It was just a throw-away, he said."

Whatever the case may be it is a fact that half of the song did indeed get thrown away. Even the title got shortened as it lost its original, parenthetic subtitle – "(The Miller's Tale)". Matthew Fisher takes up the story:

"When I joined Procol the others had already been rehearsing it for a while. It was very long, four verses. To condense it a bit we first cut out the third verse, which was obviously not as good as the others. Then when we eventually got to the point of recording it the second verse was scrapped too, again to reduce the length. So in fact we were left with only two verses, which were the original verses one and four. They are the official version of the song, but for some reason the original second verse was printed on the sheet music when it came out."

"A Whiter Shade Of Pale" has been described as "the greatest acid lyric ever written" and it has often been associated with the evolving hippie scene of 1967. Reid strongly rejects all this by stating, "I had never taken acid when I wrote that song and I don't think I had done very many drugs either." So whatever "A Whiter Shade Of Pale" may be, psychedelic blabber it is not.

Over the years numerous attempts have been made to analyse the lyric and find some kind of meaning behind it. Unfortunately, it has nearly all been looking at this one song on its own as if the rest of Reid's work didn't exist at all. Likewise, there have been no attempts to incorporate into this analysis even the few details we have of Reid's personal background.

Personally, I don't believe in such analysis. If you want to know what is on Keith Reid's mind you have to start by looking at his work as a whole, and then work your way downwards from there into perhaps more subtle details.

More of which later on. At the moment it is enough to suggest that "A Whiter Shade Of Pale" deals in metaphorical form with a male/female relationship which after some negotiation ends in a sexual act. This, incidentally, is further supported by looking at the famous "missing verse" which ends with the narrator and his female friend hitting "the ocean bed". Perhaps more importantly the whole narrative, in a typical Reid-esque manner, oozes confusion, dizziness and a notion of being "lost at sea" underlined by the impression that the scenario literally takes place on board a ship.

Describing sex in a metaphorical form is one of the main features in rhythm 'n' blues lyrics. Songs like "Walking The Dog" and "Ride Your Pony" are hardly to be taken literally as representing the author's love of outdoor life in the company of some creature from the animal kingdom.

In that sense "A Whiter Shade Of Pale" is a typical R&B lyric. What makes it different, however, is the explicitly white, intellectual imagery (which has been compared with surrealist painters) and the employment of a vocabulary that couldn't be much further removed from Ray Charles or Leiber & Stoller. In Paul Carter's interview Gary Brooker recalled his first impressions on seeing the lyric:

"There was always something special about all Keith's words. On the other hand, this was nice because it was an epic. Each verse was very long when you see it written on paper. This was a full-up A4 masterpiece. Some of them were short five or six liners, two verses and a chorus; but this was a mammoth thing. I was immediately interested. I read through it once when it arrived in the post and thought, 'Oh, this is fantastic.' I read it and then put it on the piano."

As in several other interviews on the writing of "A Whiter Shade Of Pale" Brooker then continues to refer to a jazz version of the Bach composition "Air On A G String" released as a single in 1966 by noted French pianist Jacques Loussier and his trio. In one of my own interviews with Brooker, he described the writing process as follows:

"I sat down one day and perhaps I was trying to play it ['Air On A G String'], and I just started off on the bass line and I put some chords with the right. I think only the first four notes are the same, then it starts to change. I sang a tune over the top. I thought the in-between would have some theme, which I wrote."

The mesmerising nature of the song is partly created by what seems like an ever descending bass line.

"What the bass notes were doing was to me very important," Brooker said. "If it was an E-chord they played an 'e', and when it went up to A it played 'a', or around there. But I started to find out that the whole nature of a chord changed with the bass note that you had with it..."

In keeping with the tradition of all great pop records the writing of the music for "A Whiter Shade Of Pale" seems to have been done in less than half an hour. Gary Brooker again:

"Once I got the idea that you just keep playing these chords descending I just went round and round. I was there. The only problem was that I thought, 'How am I going to get to the repeated bit at the end of every verse?' And so I just banged in this triplet, just changed the tempo of the chords for a bar, then carried on with the chords again. You just have to flip it round at the end of the last line so that you start again."[11]

A point Brooker fails to mention is that in order to put an end to the ever descending bass line he had to incorporate a tried and tested pop song cadence for the final line of the chorus (Buddy Holly in particular was fond of this cadence and used it in songs such as "Peggy Sue" and "I'm Gonna Love You Too", both part of The Paramounts' repertoire). It is by employing tricks of this kind – and by performing the song largely within a rhythm 'n' blues framework – that Brooker manages to set Reid's lyric fully to music. Indeed, to anyone who might have thought rhythm 'n' blues and baroque music were like the proverbial chalk and cheese, "A Whiter Shade Of Pale" must have come as quite a surprise. Whatever you think of the song, it does not sound fragmented.

In the beginning it didn't occur to the composers themselves that this was a tune with any hit potential at all. It is easy to understand why. There are a few slightly adventurous features, such as the way the melody stretches the chord at the beginning of the chorus (a similar effect was used the following year by The Hollies on "Carrie Ann"). Also, the complete lack of syncopation, which is highly unusual for what in many respects is a rock song. However, that isn't enough to disguise the fact that the chord sequence is little more than a simplification of one of the most famous and loved compositions in classical music.

Nevertheless, "A Whiter Shade Of Pale" managed to capture that "certain something" which turned it into one of the biggest hits in the history of popular music. More than any other Procol Harum composition it is a pop song. It immediately sucks you in from the first time you hear it, it even works as a dance floor number. Finally, it was possible to smoke strange substances, listen to the words and go to all sorts of places within ones mind.

Significantly, the first person to see the chart possibilities in "A Whiter Shade Of Pale" appears to have been bassist Dave Knights. Arguably the least theoretically trained member of the band, he intuitively sensed the song's potential, pointed it out to the others and suggested it become a single.

In the meantime the group were still struggling to get a stable line-up together. BJ Wilson had left. Richard Brown had been replaced by Ray Royer (born 8 October 1945), who had also been present at the Roebuck audition. Coming from a background of classical violin and guitar lessons Royer had, during the mid-sixties, been a member of High Time, a Mod group playing mainly Motown covers. The band supported The Searchers and also included keyboard player Malcolm Holland plus bass player Dennis Taylor, who went on to play with Arthur Brown.

For some time Royer and Knights rehearsed as a trio in the church hall with Gary Brooker, while still advertising for a drummer and an organ player. But no organist could be found, and the drummers who turned up in general proved to be a headache. "We went through a month or so of constantly changing them," Brooker told Paul Carter.

One thing that made the concept of Procol Harum unique right from the start, at least in the UK, was the intention to include two keyboards in the line-up.

"We wanted an organ player," Brooker told me. "Someone with a Hammond. We specifically wanted that sound of both a piano and an organ, which was a bit of a luxury in those days."

Even more than a luxury, having two keyboards in the same band was quite simply unheard of in England at the time. The only group with that sort of instrumental line-up seems to have been Bob Dylan's backing band, later known simply as The Band. They toured the UK in 1966 – Brooker and Reid were there in the audience. (The fact that The Band's organist, Garth Hudson, used a Lowrey organ was perhaps something they weren't aware of. They were totally focused on finding themselves a keyboard player with a Hammond.)

There is little doubt that Dylan was a strong influence on particularly Reid and Stevens around this time. Everyone who had any contact with the group mentions this. Richard Brown recalled them playing *Highway 61* – ad nauseam.

Hammond organs were very expensive; people owning and playing them were few and far between. Brooker, Reid and Stevens had already advertised for organ players for some time without much luck. Then they discovered that there was a Hammond player advertising in *Melody Maker* too, looking for jobs.

"Matthew advertised," Keith Reid told me. "We saw his advert... It was magic finding him. He was just such a fantastic musician. It was unbelievable that we found him. Definitely a bit of magic that our paths crossed."

Second take, no overdubs

We were all poor. The feeling was that we would probably break up after this one record. If it made it, okay. If it didn't, goodbye.

Gary Brooker [12]

Matthew Charles Fisher was born 7 March 1946 and has lived nearly all his life in Croydon, South London. Both his parents were musically inclined – his mother played a bit of piano, his father played guitar and ukulele and was a jazz fan. The father furthermore had ambitions to become a writer and published short stories in magazines under the pseudonym of Christina Blake.

Matthew started having piano lessons at a young age together with his sister, Judith. However, his interest in music was mainly on a theoretical level.

"When I was very young I had this dream of myself becoming some sort of great classical composer, which didn't really, ahem, happen," he told me. "Though I had these classical piano lessons as a child I was too lazy to do anything proper about it."

As Matthew grew older he found more joy in playing with bands at school. He started as a rhythm guitarist in a Shadows inspired line-up, Matt and the Deputies, then switched to bass as the group changed its name to Society Five. After leaving school Fisher advertised in the music papers for jobs as a bass player. Nothing happened.

"In those days bass players weren't supposed to play that well, but they *were* supposed to look good. So all people wanted when it came to bass players was image, which I never had much of, I suppose."

Then Matthew Fisher discovered that there was a great demand for organists. This was around 1964-65, when The Animals and Georgie Fame were high in the charts. So he got himself a cheap Vox organ and after that never had any problems getting work in bands.

After having played with different groups for a while Fisher became a student at the Guildhall School of Music. However, he left after one year only.

"I didn't like the idea of becoming a music teacher, and it seemed to be the only thing this line of education would lead me into. Instead I joined various professional line-ups, like The Gamblers. They were a Newcastle group who used to back Billy Fury."

Billy Fury and The Gamblers did a tour with The John Barry Seven, whose bass player Stan Haldane told me:

"Matthew really stuck out in that line-up. The Gamblers were a bunch of hardened Geordies, and he looked so young and innocent – he was straight out of music school at that time. Every time there was a break of some sort he'd sit there at his organ and play classical stuff. We saw ourselves as real rock 'n' rollers so we found that quite amusing. But both personality-wise and because he was such a great player he gradually won us all over, and by the end of the tour no one was laughing, I can guarantee that. Then we didn't see him for a while and suddenly one day he was on TV with Gary Brooker and they had this great big hit. We all shouted, 'Look – it's him, it's Matthew!' It was great to see him do so well."

Geoff Bannister (keyboard player with The John Barry Seven) recalls that, "There was this thing about Matthew – he had two Vox organs, stacked on top of one another! Or perhaps it was just one of the first two-manual Vox organs in this country he had, I'm not sure. But I used to be really impressed - this guy was so good that one organ wasn't enough for him, he needed to have two!"

After leaving The Gamblers, Fisher went through a succession of other line-ups for a while.

"I was in The Downliners Sect for about a week," he said. "And also in Peter Jay and the Jaywalkers when they were backing Paul Jones and had Terry Reid on guitar."

The Jaywalkers played a package tour in 1966 with The Hollies and The Small Faces. This was where Fisher had his first one-to-one encounter with the mighty Hammond organ.

"Ian McLagan [of The Small Faces] had a Hammond and I could never keep my fingers away from it. I kept going, 'Can I have a go at your Hammond, please?' all day until in the end he'd had enough. 'They're yelling out for Hammond players,' he said, 'why don't you go out and buy one for yourself?'"

Fisher agreed and with some help from his grandmother managed to raise the deposit for a Hammond M102, a so-called "tone wheel" organ.

The characteristic Hammond sound was essential to Procol Harum throughout most of their career, so it might be appropriate to explain a little bit about these organs and what makes them stand out from all other electric keyboard instruments.

Unlike normal electric organs, Hammond's "tone wheel" models work according to a unique system where the sound is produced by cogwheels rotating in front of electromagnets, inducing an alternating current which is sent through various electric filters and then amplified. With lots of mechanical parts moving inside it, an up-and-steaming Hammond shivers slightly and feels almost alive.

More importantly (and unlike modern-day synthesisers, samplers and so forth) Hammonds also *sound* totally alive. However, to make a Hammond sound *really* good you need a Lesley cabinet featuring – believe it or not – internal motors and rotating loudspeakers.

The original Hammond organs went out of production some time in the early seventies, but even today they still feature heavily in the sound of many records and younger bands such as JTQ, The Charlatans, Corduroy and Kula Shaker.

After acquiring his Hammond, Matthew Fisher soon started advertising for jobs in the *Melody Maker*. "The phone never stopped ringing. Having a Hammond was like having a licence to print money."

At the time when he was first approached by Brooker and Reid, Fisher was a member of The Savages, a backing group for Screaming Lord Sutch. The job included going on stage every night dressed as a Roman soldier and playing alongside guitarist Ritchie Blackmore.

Brooker and Reid arranged to come down to see Matthew Fisher in Croydon where he was still living with his mother and his sister, his father having passed away some two years before.

"They had this tape with them which they left with me. It was a demo of 'Salad Days', just piano and voice, pretty badly recorded. But the song itself I was impressed with. It seemed to deal with a relationship gone wrong, which was something I could quite easily identify with. Then they started talking about how big they were going to be, like bigger than The Beatles and that sort of crap. I joined them, but I still kept being a member of Lord Sutch's group, at least for a while."

One of the songs rehearsed in those stark winter days of early 1967 was, of course, "A Whiter Shade Of Pale".

"The original four verse version took around ten minutes to play," Fisher recalled, "and in between were these instrumental bits which Gary and I used to take turns to play. We just improvised at that point. Later, when we went into the studio and cut the song down to two verses, it was decided that only I should do the soloing and I kind of picked out the best pieces of what I had been improvising and turned it into more of a real theme, if you like, though still with some space for improvisation."

The organ melody which opens the song and later is repeated between the verses and at the end was roughly a combination of two compositions by Bach, "Air On A G String" and "Sleepers Awake". However, both themes had to be changed and elaborated on to fit the chord progression.

During this period the idea was that Guy Stevens and Keith Reid should work as co-managers for the group, but some kind of disagreement appears to have emerged between them. Nevertheless, Stevens arranged two demo sessions of "A Whiter Shade Of Pale".

At this point the group seemed to have found their drummer in "Tubs Drubs" (real name long forgotten).

The first session was recorded straight on to mono. Guy Stevens then came back and told the band to do another one on four-track master tape; he apparently wanted to try some different studio techniques. However, that second session wasn't as good as the first.

The controversies between Keith Reid and Guy Stevens came to a head during the days after the recording of the demos, and as a result Guy Stevens left.

Instead the demo brought the group to the attention of hip and successful producer Denny Cordell. He was mainly working independently from an office in the Essex Music office building in Denmark Street. Essex Music was run by David Platz, a major music publisher who Brooker-Reid were already signed to as songwriters. Platz had teamed up with Denny Cordell to form an independent company with the intention of producing records. Thus Brooker-Reid got in touch with Cordell. He set up a record deal for them via his own company, Straight Ahead Productions, who leased their material to various labels.

At this point Straight Ahead Productions had a contract running with Decca, though not for long. All in all, this intricate situation explains why "A Whiter Shade Of Pale" in the UK was released on the Decca sub-label Deram while the group's following releases were on EMI subsidiary Regal Zonophone.

Cordell had previously produced major hits for musicians like Georgie Fame ("Yeah Yeah") and The Moody Blues ("Go Now"). The son of a rich South American landowner he was not primarily in the business for the money. By the time he entered the history of Procol Harum, Cordell was in his early twenties, spoke without a foreign accent (in fact, he is remembered for sounding distinctively English, like Terry-Thomas), and seemed to communicate well with people from all walks of life. He wasn't a musician himself but had some controversial ideas about production.

One of Cordell's close associates during this time was Welshman Mike Lease, who later became the keyboard player of Procol Harum-offspring Freedom.

"Primarily Cordell was always looking for a sound," Lease told me. "He could create a great atmosphere in the studio and though he never intervened with the musicians' way of playing he nevertheless managed to always end up getting things the way he wanted them. I worked with some pretty special people during those years, including Denny Laine, The Move, Iain Matthews and Jimmy Page. I'd say that of all the people I knew then who were non-musicians Cordell was the one who impressed me the most."

Working as an independent producer Denny Cordell didn't follow the normal pattern for British record producers at the time. Basically he would spend a lot more time in the studio and he was very into picking up new acts.

One such act was Procol Harum, who once again found themselves without a suitable drummer. Listening to the demo Denny Cordell had decided that "Tubs" wasn't good enough.

"The session was booked and we didn't have a drummer!" Keith Reid remembered. "Denny Cordell wanted to get Mitch Mitchell, which we all really liked the idea of, but he couldn't get him."

By now, everyone was coming up with suggestions for a new drummer and an audition was held. Eventually the choice fell on Bobby Harrison, the Southend resident who had occasionally sat in for Mick Brownlee back in The Paramounts days. It appears that Harrison only joined Procol Harum the day before they made the hit single.

"I remember going with them to the studio where we were going to record," he said. "It was at the Olympic Studios in Barnes and when we arrived there was also this studio drummer that Cordell had booked, Bill Eyden. What happened was that they played the song through with him while I was sitting on a chair watching them, so that I could get an idea of how the song should be played."

The reason why Bill Eyden knew the song already was that he had heard the demo with "Tubs" playing. Denny Cordell had booked a three-hour session. "A Whiter Shade Of Pale" was recorded quickly. Two takes were enough, and no overdubs were needed.

With one song down on tape, the question was what to do with the rest of the studio time. Astonishingly, no one seems to have seriously considered what to record for the B-side, but it was suggested the band try a song called "Alpha", which was particularly well-suited to Bill Eyden's style. However, this recording never got released until 1998 when it appeared as a bonus track on Westside's CD version of the *Shine On Brightly* LP. Matthew Fisher:

"Then some days later, when we had rehearsed some more with Bobby Harrison, we asked Denny Cordell if we could go back into the studio and re-record 'A Whiter Shade Of Pale', and he agreed. That was done at Advision Studios and that was also when we recorded the B-side, 'Lime Street Blues'."

At a quick glance "Lime Street Blues" appears to be a pretty straight-forward R&B song. However, a closer look reveals some surprising similarities with "A Whiter Shade Of Pale". There is a descending bass line running underneath the melody, and each verse is interrupted by a few bars of instrumental playing, with some excellent soloing shifting between piano and organ. Arguably one of the first three tunes Brooker ever wrote with Keith Reid (the other two being "Something Following Me" and "Alpha"), "Lime Street Blues" is one of a small handful of songs which stylistically link The Paramounts and Procol Harum.

Again, the lyric sees the narrator looking to engage himself in sexual activities, though on this occasion it is more blatantly explained without any use of metaphors. Running up and down Lime Street (a real street in Liverpool frequented by prostitutes) in his underpants he for some reason gets pushed over and arrested, after which he ends up in court.

The last verse is perhaps best described as "Comicbook Kafka". The courtroom scenery is like a parody and, as in Franz Kafka's famous novel *The Trial*, we are given no real description of the crime involved. Likewise the outcome of the court case is not revealed – which all goes to emphasise that the only important issue here is the narrator's own sense of guilt. He tries to trick his way out of the situation, but the judge sees through him. When the narrator begs for mercy on his "golden locks", the judge replies sarcastically that he is not a genuine blonde, perhaps meaning "you are dishonest", a "fake".

While the situation surrounding the recording of the "A Whiter Shade Of Pale" single may appear to have been rather confusing, no one in fact was more confused than Bobby Harrison:

"I wasn't informed of what was going on behind the scenes and which decisions were made. As far as I knew we were going to release the version with me playing, so when the record came out I was actually convinced it was me playing on it. I thought I was Number 1 in the charts! Then of course I was told it was Bill Eyden and it felt, well, pretty strange."

Mike Lease explains that, "I was probably the first outside person ever to hear 'A Whiter Shade Of Pale'. I was meeting Denny Cordell at some office in Oxford Street and he was completely over the moon about this unknown act he had just recorded. He kept repeating that the song would go straight to Number 1. I said, 'Oh yeah? Put it on.' So he played me the tape. I honestly couldn't see what he was talking about and I told him so. I said, 'It won't even make it into the Top 40.' We even made a bet on it. I not only lost the money of course, I also lost my confidence in my own ability to judge a song's hit potential."

The released version of "A Whiter Shade Of Pale"/"Lime Street Blues" was mixed in mono only. There was some worry over the sound as the drummer had been hitting his cymbals very hard, creating a high-end treble problem. So Cordell decided to send an acetate copy to the pirate ship Radio London to have the song broadcast. The purpose was purely to find out what the record would sound like in people's homes. Luckily all worries were soon forgotten, the DJ announcing, "That sounds like a massive hit."

"One thing led to another and it was released," recalled Dave Knights. "To our amazement – and almost horror – it went to Number 1!"

Part Three

The golden years, 1967-1969

Problem Harum

> It was the first evening that any of us had heard Procol Harum's "A Whiter Shade Of Pale". The lyrics were all very poetic. We just thought, "God, what an incredible record!"
>
> Paul McCartney [13]

"Excuse me, have you got the new single by Procum, eh, Protocol Ha-Harem, something... ?"

"You mean Procol Harum. I'm afraid it's sold out, sir. We'll be getting in some more copies soon."

This kind of conversation was taking place in many record shops all over Britain towards the end of May 1967. From nowhere Procol Harum had gone straight into the *NME* charts at No. 11, and from there they soon leapt to Number 1.

Who were these guys? The public had to know, and the journalists set out to discover.

Apparently, Procol Harum were five fairly ordinary young men. They answered whatever questions the press were asking, drew up their musical and personal backgrounds together with all the pop trivia it was still commonplace to inquire about in those days – favourite foods, drinks, colours, current girlfriends and so forth.

High-brow university drop-outs trying to make a quick buck on the pop scene they were not, despite the rumours. In fact, none of them except their organ player had much more than compulsory schooling behind him. Instead they had all been playing rock 'n' roll for several years. Their pianist, singer and leader had even released a handful of fine singles with a band called The Paramounts.

Were they into these strange new substances everyone was talking about, LSD and so on? Not particularly. What was on their mind? Apparently nothing special.

If they were just trying to be evasive, the members of Procol Harum must have succeeded well. Commenting on the group's enormous sales figures *New Musical Express* had to resort to headlines like:

IT'S NUMBER 1! DECCA'S FASTEST SELLING SINGLE EVER! BUT... PROCOL JUST WANT TO EAT AND SLEEP!

The speed and scale of the success was almost inconceivable, even by today's standards. Three weeks after its release "A Whiter Shade Of Pale" was close to having sold its first half a million copies. In England alone the sales figure was 356,000 – in France 120,000 copies had gone over the counters in just ten days.

A calm and cross-legged Gary Brooker received the representatives of the press, divulging to them how busy he was. Photo sessions, radio sessions and interviews were taking up all his time these days. What Brooker was wise enough not to inform the press about was the extreme pressure his group was under from internal difficulties. Any success of this kind must be followed up immediately or you lose the momentum, but it was becoming more and more obvious that everything had happened much too fast for Procol Harum.

Three weeks after "A Whiter Shade Of Pale" had gone to Number 1 in the UK, the media were informed that all British dates had suddenly been cancelled because the members of Procol Harum were "mentally and physically exhausted". According to the press release the whole group had been "examined by a doctor and advised to take immediate rest".

"That was all Denny Cordell's idea," Matthew Fisher told me. "He pulled us off the road because he felt we were playing too many gigs for too little money and he wanted to put us in the studio. On top of that we got kind of stuck in the middle, we fell between two chairs, it seemed. First people heard the single and thought we were some kind of straightforward pop band, like The Tremeloes. Then they found out we were an underground band and dismissed us for that, but at the same time the underground wouldn't accept us because we had this huge pop hit."

The B-side of that huge pop hit, "Lime Street Blues", featured some fine drumming from Bobby Harrison (born 28 June 1943), who was already an experienced player when he joined Procol Harum. In the late fifties he had been a member of the above-mentioned Romford group The Rockerfellas, following which he was in several other line-ups including Golden Apples Of The Sun, who released a single ("Monkey Time") on the Immediate label in 1965, and Powerpack, who did two singles for CBS in 1966 and 1967.

Neither Harrison nor Ray Royer were the hopeless players they have sometimes been made out to be. According to Gary Brooker, "Royer had a nice vibrato, but he went blank in the studio". Bobby Harrison told me, "Ray had his moments of genius, but he was very inconsistent in those days, very nervous. It worked much better for him later when he and I formed Freedom."

Nevertheless, the general notion seems to have been that the line-up didn't gel properly. As Matthew Fisher puts it, "There was a lot of inequality in the group in the early days. Something would come up and it would be Gary and Keith off in a corner, whispering."

In retrospect it is easy enough to see that while Harrison and Royer were competent enough to be in a psychedelic pop band – which appears to be the right description for Procol Harum in their earliest days – there were other ambitions in the back of the minds of Brooker and Reid. To really revolutionise rock 'n' roll and get the best out of the songs they were writing together a different kind of player was called for.

"I remember the early line-up playing gigs with Jimi Hendrix," said Matthew Fisher. "We were top of the bill with Hendrix billed below us. No way were we one tenth as good as him at the time, and the only reason we didn't get booed off was probably that we were Number 1 that week. There was certainly some raised eyebrows on that occasion."

With Guy Stevens out of the picture[14], Procol Harum now landed Jonathan Weston as their manager. He was running New Breed Management together with Denny Cordell. However, it appears that there was some kind of disagreement between the two, and some of the band members certainly weren't pleased with Weston's way of conducting things.

When the group went into the studio to record an album and a follow-up to their hit single, the pressures were extreme. Harrison and particularly Royer seem to have suffered more than the others. Consequently, the tracks recorded during these sessions were utterly awful. Considering that the drummer and guitarist later the very same year made a really good soundtrack LP as members of the now legendary and highly collectable Freedom, displaying considerable abilities not only as musicians but also as songwriters, it is hard to believe we are even talking about the same people.

The first Procol Harum line-up got as far as recording what roughly amounts to half an LP. So far a version of "Salad Days (Are Here Again)" has been included as a bonus-track on a CD of Procol Harum's first eponymous album on Westside Records, which also erroneously credits a later version of "Cerdes (Outside The Gates Of)" to the same line-up.

In fact, "Cerdes" *was* recorded during these sessions but remains unreleased along with similar early versions of "Kaleidoscope", "Something Following Me", "She Wandered Through The Garden Fence" and "A Christmas Camel". Furthermore, an alternative take of "In The Wee Small Hour Of Sixpence", which regularly pops up on compilation LPs and CDs, sounds as if it features Bobby Harrison on drums (no guitar can be heard).

I remember listening to acetates of the above outtakes with Gary Brooker and being taken aback by the quality of his singing on these tracks. Some of them were even better vocal performances than the splendid final versions featured on the official LP recorded a few months later, and likewise the Hammond playing is, as you would expect, truly magnificent. However, it is my view that there is no way these recordings could ever have been released at the time.

Was it an act of panic when Procol Harum – arguably under strong influence from Denny Cordell – suddenly sacked both their manager and two of their members? Could it all have been done in a more considerate way without giving parts of the press the opportunity to severely damage the rest of the group's career in their homeland?

There don't seem to have been any obvious alternatives to what Brooker and Reid did at the time. Whichever way you look at it

Procol Harum were truly and utterly stuck in a jam at the height of the success of "A Whiter Shade Of Pale". What should have been the greatest moment of their lives had almost immediately turned into a genuine Keith Reid-esque nightmare of being unable to find your direction, of feeling under pressure and perhaps even physically unwell while there's a crowd around you calling out for more.

However, the problems didn't end there. Keith Reid explained that, "There was all this thing about what the name meant... These were all things that came up after we were successful. We never knew Procol Harum had any Latin derivation or it might mean this or it might mean that. If we'd known about all that we'd been a lot cleverer."

Answering that the name came from a cat belonging to some friend of a former co-manager didn't make matters much clearer – and even people who *did* know Latin complained that the term Procol Harum made no sense.

Eventually the cat's birth certificate had to be produced - since it was a pedigree Burmese cat such a thing actually existed. It then turned out that the spelling should have been Procul Harun[15] apparently meaning something like "beyond these things" – not wholly inappropriate for a band supposedly epitomising the "Spirit of 1967".

The problem was that by now Procol Harum was an established name and changing the spelling would only have made matters worse. Also Procul Harun for some reason didn't really sound like much of a band name.

So it was a classic no-win situation. Whatever the group did, it couldn't change the impression some people had that they were trying to be cleverer than they were, giving their band some strange Latin name without being able to spell it right.

"A Whiter Shade Of Pale" hadn't been in the charts long before drummer Bill Eyden arrived on the scene with a demand that he be paid royalties for the recording. So far, all he had been given was his normal session player's fee.

In some parts of the press this caused quite a stir which apparently continues to this very day (as late as 1998 a major British music magazine managed to run the story once again as if it were a huge sensation). I asked for an inside view on the issue from Mike Lease, who was working steadily as a session player for Denny Cordell at the time.

"The positive thing about being a session musician is that you always get paid a fixed, agreed sum for your work," Lease said. "If a record flops – even if it never comes out – the session player still gets his money. You're a hired hand. The downside is, of course, that you aren't paid any sales royalties.

"Working for Cordell was a great privilege, he treated us well and he paid us handsomely. In most cases we earned a lot more money than people generally got from playing in bands. Since bands split their performance royalties between themselves it meant that you could play on a session and if the song became a hit the person you had been sitting in for got the performance royalties. But that was the name of the game, we all knew that."

It sounds unlikely that Bill Eyden was unaware of these terms when he entered the studio to record with Procol Harum. He was a very experienced player. Nevertheless, these appear to have been the terms he now protested against. Whether he had a point or not people must decide for themselves, but it definitely didn't do much good for Procol Harum to be at the centre of what appeared to be Eyden's battle to revolutionise session players' working conditions.

Keith Reid stated, "It was all a load of rubbish. He was a session drummer, he was booked for a session, he played on the session. I think the press tried to make something out of it that it wasn't. I can remember that it did us a lot of harm at the time."

The next problematic situation arrived when Matthew Fisher, by his own account, approached Brooker and suggested he be granted a percentage of the composing royalties for the music on "A Whiter Shade Of Pale". Matthew Fisher claims to have felt – particularly after seeing the published sheet music for the song – that his contribution to the record was such a considerable feature that it entitled him to some kind of a share. According to Matthew Fisher, Gary Brooker blankly refused. The organist replied that he would leave the band.

I have never seen or heard Brooker publicly comment directly on this matter, and even if he had it would still be very much outside the framework of this biography to take anyone's side in such disputes. What remains to be reported is that according to at least two sources (Robin Trower and Matthew Fisher) Procol Harum over the next two and a half years found themselves in a situation of constant internal uncertainty, where one of their essential members was not only regularly threatening to leave them, but in fact actually did go his own way on several occasions – and was then persuaded to come back again.

It is significant that Matthew Fisher's recollections of being in Procol Harum during the group's first few months are clear down to the most minute detail. He recalls exactly what Keith Reid said to him the very first time they spoke on the phone, even his tone of voice. He recalls lyrics down to the last comma or punctuation mark.

However, sometime shortly after the release of "A Whiter Shade Of Pale" it all seems to get rather blurred. Did the early line-up tour Scandinavia? Matthew Fisher isn't sure. When exactly were Harrison and Royer told to leave the group? Not entirely sure either. Where was the audition held for new players? Can't remember.

"I went through a terrible patch," he explained. "The band had problems, I had this dispute with Gary, plus I was losing my girlfriend at the time, and furthermore I hadn't managed to get over the death of my father two years earlier. Then one day I smoked one joint too many and almost suffered a breakdown of some kind. Later, in Stockholm, I got flashbacks from that event and had to be taken to a hospital there."

There doesn't seem to have been much fun in "the Summer of Love" for Matthew Fisher. He once said to me, regretfully, "Procol Harum were never a happy band." Perhaps that sums things up pretty well, though it must be seen in connection with Fisher's statements about his own personal situation at the time. He doesn't exactly claim to have been the world's most uplifting company.

Welcome back, my friends

They should have been a bit more cool about it. It was just a mess. They had the chance to be one of the big Top 5 groups in the world, and they blew it.

Robin Trower

It is difficult to pin down who exactly was responsible for the chaos surrounding Procol Harum during the success of "A Whiter Shade Of Pale". Several people involved – including Matthew Fisher and Bobby Harrison – put the blame blame mainly on Denny Cordell, who apparently had developed a strong personal dislike for Harrison. It also seems that Cordell was convinced Procol Harum was a sinking ship. There was a feeling within the band that he didn't put in enough time and energy, and there was even a point when he tried to make BJ Wilson leave them and join Joe Cocker instead. Keith Reid:

"We weren't listening to other people's perception of us; we were very, very busy. We were trying to consolidate the success of the record. We were really in demand. We were just doing TV shows here and there and trying to make a record. We were just so busy. If we had been paying attention to what other people thought we would have done things a lot differently... We weren't very calculating. We weren't objective at all... We thought that it was simple. You just made a record and played on stage."

With Harrison and Royer out of the group the search started for a new guitarist and a drummer. Gary Brooker didn't have to look far.

Since leaving The Paramounts prior to their German tour with Chris Andrews in the autumn of 1966, Robin Trower had gone back to Southend. Here he first tried forming a band with guitarist Wilko Johnson. But Johnson had decided to stop playing in groups and go to university instead (he returned in the early seventies to become a member of Dr Feelgood). Instead, Trower went on to form a blues/rock trio called The Jam (obviously no relation to the late 70's punk band of the same name). He asked BJ Wilson to join this line-up, but he declined.

In June or July, Trower received a phone call from Gary Brooker who asked if he would be interested in auditioning for Procol Harum. Robin Trower recalled Procol Harum being under a lot of pressure when he joined. To sack two group members and bring in a couple of old friends instead certainly didn't diminish the criticism in the press. Robin Trower:

"I think it was the right thing to do, but on the other hand it didn't look good to the media, the fact that they changed two members right when they were Number 1. I remember Gary told me that he saw Mick Jagger at the time that all that was going down, and Jagger said to him, 'You've blown it.' He was right, they *had* blown it."

Perhaps it should be emphasised that Robin Trower's criticism does not include the band's artistic situation. In fact, he was impressed with the way Brooker had developed as a songwriter:

"It was interesting, very experimental. For me it was, anyway. Some of the songs were very good, quite soulful, one or two quite bluesy. It was just too good an opportunity to miss."

By the autumn of 1966, BJ Wilson had, as previously mentioned, become a member of George Bean & The Runners. He had also played in a psychedelic group called The Sands. Furthermore, he was for a while a member of Freddie Mack's Boss Sound, a band which included Wilson's old school-pal and future fellow Procol Harum bass player, Alan George Cartwright.

Freddie Mack reputedly saw himself as Britain's answer to James Brown. The band toured extensively during the sixties, interrupted by residencies at the Upper Cut, a London club run by the boxer Billy Walker. Alan Cartwright:

"Freddie Mack was really successful, simply because people wanted to hear the record they liked reproduced by a 'live' band. But it had no class or style about it. How long was I in it? Too bloody long."[16]

Things didn't quite work out for Freddie Mack; in fact there was so little money in the band that Wilson at one point complained he couldn't afford to buy drumsticks any more. Freddie Mack only shrugged at this, and consequently BJ Wilson played the next gig with only one stick.

On the whole Wilson's activities between September 1966 and June 1967 are a pretty shambolic affair. When I talked to him during a Joe Cocker tour in the early eighties he told me, "You'd need ten tapes to explain that. I was doing other things. Gary was writing and I'd always see him and see Keith, you know... I was off touring when they actually started making records."

The fact is that sometime in June or July 1967, BJ Wilson had a similar phone call to the one Robin Trower received, and the two of them went in to London to audition. Everyone was immediately struck by Wilson's playing abilities, Dave Knights in particular:

"It was quite an experience to play with BJ Wilson. I was used to very straight drummers and he used to do all these fancy trick beats and things, delaying different passages and then coming in."

Out of the two guitarists at the audition Robin Trower proved to be the better. As Gary Brooker recalled:

"When Keith and Guy and I got together – and we were talking about getting a band together ourselves to do the songs – that is the way we'd thought it and we were very lucky with the people we found and the way it turned out. To have this good solid background, you know, big organ sound, something where people could solo, and a blues guitar over the top – where there was always room for solos, but whenever somebody soloed there was a lot of strength behind it all the time with the chords and the bass. And also to have that type of guitar wandering through a much more interesting background of chords... "

On 15 July 1967 the *New Musical Express* announced that, with sales of "A Whiter Shade Of Pale" now exceeding 2.5 million copies world-wide, two group members had left the Procol Harum camp to be replaced by lead guitarist Robin Trower and drummer Barrie Wilson, both ex-members of Gary Brooker's former group, The Paramounts. Furthermore Tony Secunda had been appointed the group's co-manager (along with Keith Reid), replacing Jonathan Weston. Though the new line-up was now a fact, there would be no Procol Harum tour of Britain until the autumn. Instead the band was planning to visit six countries in mainland Europe.

What the papers didn't know was that Matthew Fisher in the meantime had left the group. Robin Trower:

"It was only because I talked him into it that he stayed on... I had to go down to his house and convince him that it was worth staying on, that we should do this American tour and this and that and all the rest of the old cobblers."

The first record to be released following Trower and Wilson's arrival was "Homburg", featuring yet another highly unusual lyric by Keith Reid.

Reid's early work can be divided into two categories, with some overlapping. The first category contains songs which appear to have been written as a "stream of consciousness" and include numerous images of a surreal nature. They often employ an abundance of characters, some of them mythological, others self-invented.

The second category of songs deals in a more direct form with a feeling of futility, lack of direction, depression and resignation, of living in a dreamy half-world where everything is scattered and fragmented.

"Homburg" mainly belongs in the first category, though some of the vocabulary and imagery also fits into the second. In the song's second verse, for instance, we are told that old guides like the sun and the moon will soon start to "shudder", and that some signpost will "cease to sign". Furthermore there is mentioned a clock which is no longer giving the right time – all images spiritually belonging into the second category.

Some of this imagery is reminiscent of "A Whiter Shade Of Pale", with its dreamy dimness and an overall feeling of helplessness. Indeed, the song on its release was criticised for being too close to its predecessor.

Such criticism could also be applied to the formal structure of the lyric, which is almost exactly the same as on the first single. Moreover, the two records have striking similarities in tempo and arrangement.

"Homburg" is a fine song and a good performance, but it lacks the penetrating power which turned "A Whiter Shade Of Pale" into a Number 1 hit. The piano theme is no match for the organ theme on the first single, and perhaps just as importantly the song's chorus seems to insist on building up to a climax which isn't indicated in the lyric. Keith Reid:

"We wanted our second single to be bigger than our first one. We had 'Conquistador' at that time, and in retrospect *that* should have been the second single and it probably would have been a much bigger hit than 'Homburg'."

There are several recorded versions of "Homburg" in circulation, indicating that putting the song down on tape might have been a painful process. It has even been claimed that an earlier version featuring Bobby Harrison and Ray Royer eventually had to be used. When I put this to BJ Wilson, he answered:

"When we did 'Homburg' I went in and played to the finished track because the drums were really strange on it. There wasn't anything wrong, it just wasn't right. So I went in and actually played over what he'd been playing."

This statement is consistent with Matthew Fisher's recollection of the event – in fact, he claims that Wilson only added a few drum rolls to the already existing recording with Harrison on drums. In contrast, the common perception still seems to be that this is a straight-forward Procol Harum "Mark II" recording which has nothing to do with the early line-up.

Whatever the case may be, this whole situation sounds suspiciously like yet another moment of panic on board the Harum ship during the summer of 1967.

Meanwhile, the problems with the press continued.

"When 'Homburg' made it to number 5 it was seen as a big fiasco for us," recalled Matthew Fisher. "Then soon after The Herd made it to the same position with their new single and it was apparently a great sensation."

It can't have been comforting for the band to realise that even with Trower and Wilson things weren't quite working out. Nevertheless it was felt that Procol Harum had finally found a well-balanced line-up and work started on re-recording the group's first album.

Meanwhile, in the midst of all this, "A Whiter Shade Of Pale" kept selling all over the world. And selling, and selling, and selling. As it has done practically ever since.

Medieval spacemen

We recorded it so quickly. I think we did five tracks in one day. It was
totally a "live" record.

Keith Reid

Procol Harum spent a week during the late summer of 1967 in a
recording studio. Here was the group who had the largest-selling single of the year, a record that would change music history forever. You
would think they deserved more than a week to record an entire
album. You would think they deserved more than four tracks to record
it on, and a stereo mix to be released along with the mono version.

Denny Cordell didn't think so. And neither do I, incidentally. It is a
well-known fact that The Beatles had spent a lot of time over the previous year working on their *Sgt. Pepper* album. But the songs Keith
Reid and Gary Brooker had been writing so far weren't really experimental in the same manner as The Beatles were at the time. Ground-
breaking they were, but they still had one foot solidly planted in the
established British style of R&B, and that style of music is always
best recorded on a tight schedule.

There were influences from the baroque tradition in Gary Brooker's
compositions, both in the chord sequences, the bass lines and the
almost mathematical melody lines. Nevertheless, his songs at this
point in many respects continued to have more in common with
Georgie Fame than with Bach or Handel. Also, Matthew Fisher's

organ playing had more in common with Jimmy Smith than the classics. All in all, the classical aspect was the stepchild who had been adopted into the rhythm 'n' blues family, not the other way around.

"I only knew the pop classics," Brooker told me, confirming this view. "I mean, I don't know any obscure pieces of classical music. 'Air On A G String' for instance, I only knew that because it was used in the advert for Hamlet Cigars!"

With regard to the mono/stereo debate it is enough to look at most of the other British beat group albums released in stereo at the time, including The Beatles' records, nearly all of which suffer from truly horrible stereo separation. Placing the drums on one side and the vocals on the other doesn't really make for integrated listening at all. Give me glorious mono any old time.

The first Procol Harum album has a reputation for poor sound quality and primitive production, but that primarily seems to relate to foreign pressings which were often strangely boosted in the mid-range by cutting engineers or even "re-channelled" into simulated stereo. These pressings are practically a crime against the music of the group, but even the original UK mono version sounds a bit tinny, particularly with the vocals, and lacks lower bass. Current CD issues are much better. I would particularly recommend the 1998 UK release by Westside.

Procol Harum was released in a simple black and white art sleeve with no photographs of the group, the front depicting a young girl in a forest standing underneath a tree. Responsible for this drawing was Keith Reid's girlfriend Dickinson, whom he later married. For some reason the record company felt that the tree in the drawing needed more leaves to fill out the upper right hand side of the picture, so they added some themselves. These can easily be spotted as they are about twice the size of Dickinson's original leaves.

The back of the sleeve gives only the most basic information such as who wrote the songs, the names of the players and the producer (Denny Cordell), plus a track listing. We are also reminded to listen to the record "in the spirit in which it was made". What the sleeve fails to mention is that the album was recorded at three London studios, Advision and Olympic I and II, and engineered by Eddie Kramer and Keith Grant. Furthermore, Gary Brooker didn't just sing and play piano as stated on the sleeve, he also played celeste (on "Mabel").

The first song on the album, "Conquistador", is about losing belief
in your icons, presumably either religious or philosophical ones. The
narrator speaks directly and scornfully to his former idol, who once
set out to conquer unknown territories but instead ended up getting
washed away by the sea. The image is essential – in fact, the sea is the
most significant and frequently recurring metaphor in Reid's entire
work. My guess is that it symbolises life, something you have to cross
in order to get to "the other side" – meanwhile, you are bewildered
and without a course.

The basic ideology here – as on most of the record which to a certain extent picks up from this point – is reminiscent of post-war
European existentialism. It is also representative of the feelings that
existed in the Jewish East End community during the decades following the Second World War, where it was common among young intellectuals to ask the inevitable: if God exists, how could he allow the
holocaust to happen?

Melodically, Brooker picks up on the Spanish motif. The piano
chops out simple chords eight-to-the-bar, with guitar and bass adding
little lines in unison to link up the changes. The drums provide spo-
radic rolls, mostly following guitar and bass, while the organ flows
menacingly in the background. Then a steady Motown beat sets in for
a couple of lines followed by the explosive chorus, which is sheer
rhythm 'n' blues.

Brooker's dry, matter-of-fact delivery is emphasised by the three
verses following right after one another with no in-between break or
bridge. After the singing is over there is a short, percussive Hammond
solo, and then it's all over. Clocking in at 2:38 "Conquistador" could
have been a great single (and did indeed become one – five years
down the line).

The second track on the LP is "She Wandered Through The Garden
Fence". Like Pete Townshend's "Pictures Of Lily", written around the
same time, the lyric appears to be about masturbation. Some strange,
non-existent woman walks into the narrator's garden, grabs him by
the wrist and throws him down on his back. There is a strong notion
of sexual guilt and torment shining through Reid's vocabulary here.

The structure of the lyric is quite similar to that of both "A Whiter
Shade Of Pale" and "Homburg", but as a composer Brooker goes in a
totally different direction here. Apparently built over Edward

MacDowell's romantic piano piece "To A Wild Rose", with the organ imitating Jeremiah Clarke's "Trumpet Voluntary", the melody leaps along over a set of short, mainly descending bass lines. The line-up is augmented with a tambourine, bashed by either BJ Wilson or Rocky Didzornu, the percussionist from Denny Laine's band who helped out during the recordings. Matthew Fisher plays a rehearsed Hammond solo after the second verse in his unique Jimmy Smith-meets-Clarke style, and the solo is repeated again after Brooker's repetition of the first verse.

With its American allusions "Something Following Me" is one of the most Bob Dylan-inspired songs on the album. In a slightly ironic tone the narrator reveals his inability to escape the notion of his own death. There might also be a suicidal undertone.

This is the first song on the LP to feature a more up-front guitar. Trower hits the strings with the sound turned off and then eases the chords in with the volume control. Between the second and third verse there is a piano solo leading into a heavily distorted guitar solo played with immense feel. However, the main musical feature here – as indeed on most of the album – is the collaboration between organ and piano.

The less said about "Mabel" the better. Written originally as "a bit of a joke, a jug song for someone like the Lovin' Spoonful", and seemingly performed as an unsuccessful attempt to emulate Bob Dylan songs like "Rainy Day Women #12 & 35", this quite simply isn't funny. Considering that Brooker-Reid at the time had songs like "Pandora's Box", "Alpha" and "So Far Behind" it seems a waste that a track like this was ever allowed to appear on the record. (The fiddle, incidentally, is played by the violinist from Denny Laine's band, with the whole group along with their producer providing background noises).

Moving swiftly onwards to the closing song on side one, "Cerdes (Outside The Gates Of)". This – incidentally one of my personal Procol Harum favourites – is an all-hands-on-deck performance where the group for the first time draw fully on the qualities of the new line-up. Bass and piano introduce the song in unison with a beautiful "blue" riff, then the drums join in followed by organ and guitar. The collaboration here is mainly between these two instruments. In between the verses they both play little snippets of solos, until the

organ after the second verse pulls back to make room for an outstandingly well-constructed guitar solo.

The lyric for "Cerdes" must belong in Keith Reid's bag of "wonderful nonsense" – a collage of scattered images. Interestingly, this mode
of expression fits into the album's more general concept of confusion
and fragmentation.

Side two opens with "A Christmas Camel". The setting again is a
collage of images interspersed by a questioning of the narrator's sani-
ty, perhaps presented in a slightly vain manner. The overall feeling is
of shame, shyness and paranoia. In the last verse there is a mention of
having to hide and escape across the sea to some place full of other
exiles; an obvious inspiration from the environment Reid had grown
up in and perhaps even his own family history.

The production of this song, as of the entire album, is drenched in
Hammond organ. There is a *big* guitar solo (between the second and
the third verse in what already seems to have become a Procol Harum
tradition), but otherwise Trower's playing is inaudible.

We then arrive at what I see as the album's lyrical centrepiece,
"Kaleidoscope". With its strong overtones of disorder, disillusionment
and fragmentation the song appears to sum up pretty accurately what
Reid's work was primarily about at this point. Amid darkness and
chaos we find him longing for a sense of coherence, an all-pervading
truth. Keith Reid's existentialism and atheism is never arrogant – it is
tired, reluctant and above all regretful. Somewhere deep underneath it
is a glimpse of hope that he might actually be wrong – and sometimes
(particularly later on) there is a fear that if in fact God exists after all,
He might be evil.

The music on "Kaleidoscope" is built over a strong bass riff, with
some very percussive Hammond playing. Perhaps the ending of the
song, where Wilson, Trower and Fisher display mutual admiration for
The Who's anarchic noise-making, more than anything reflects the
deep desperation presented in the lyric.

Next up is "Salad Days (Are Here Again)". Very Dylan-esque and
once again totally Hammond-drenched this is the closest we get to a
real love song on this LP. However, as you would expect it isn't exactly about summer kisses, but concerns a severely troubled and injured
relationship. The feeling is of victimisation, gloom and helplessness.
There are quite a few songs built over such themes spread over Reid's

early production, nearly always putting the entire blame on the female part of the relationship.

Even more than normal Brooker manages to capture and enhance the mood of the lyric on "Salad Days". The music seems to be sifting out towards you from some locked-up, dusty wooden cupboard. The interaction between piano and organ underlines the immense degree of musical understanding between the two players, though I must admit to feeling rather unimpressed by Fisher's self-declared attempt to produce a solo in the style of Al Kooper.

"Good Captain Clack" had already appeared on the B-side of "Homburg" (albeit in a slightly different mix). As another stab at making a comedy song this track is less annoying than "Mabel", but still sits uncomfortably among the other songs on the LP. It has a self-mocking lyric about being too self-centred, about having to learn to resign, and a prediction that heavy drinking might be a method for the Captain to come to terms with his dissatisfaction with himself and the world.

This is a very rare example of Keith Reid not writing in the first person, but there is no reason to suggest that the song is any less autobiographical than the rest of his work. In fact, Reid for several years listed himself in the telephone directory under the name of Captain Clack. Furthermore the drinking theme recurs later on many occasions.

The album closes with "Repent Walpurgis", a powerhouse instrumental composed by Matthew Fisher. He wanted to call it "Repent", while Booker suggested "Walpurgis" – eventually they agreed just to combine the two words.

The track sums up many of the qualities Procol Harum stood for – fantastic playing, dynamics, stoic energy. It was written during the days of the Royer-Harrison line-up and based on a chord sequence Fisher had heard on a Four Seasons record. However, it wasn't until Robin Trower joined the group and stamped his distinctive blues guitar all over the track that it became the much-loved showpiece we now know.

One of the great discoveries Procol Harum made at this time was that it was possible to actually play a blues guitar solo over a set of classical chords, as long as it stuck to a minor key. It was an invention born out of necessity, since Harum was a band who were somewhat classically influenced but whose guitarist was totally devoted to playing blues music. In theory the merging of these styles looked improbable, but it nevertheless worked in practice – unlike much of the so-called Progressive Rock following in the wake of Procol Harum, where different styles often just replaced each other rather than being genuinely fused.

It was Gary Brooker who suggested the middle break to "Repent Walpurgis" where the piano quotes part of Bach's famous *Prelude No. 1 In C Major* – an astonishing ending to a fabulous debut album.

There is a reference on the sleeve of *Procol Harum* to the soundtrack from a film called *Separation*.

This project came about when film director/producer Jack Bond heard "A Whiter Shade Of Pale" on the radio and decided that he wanted "the sound of that organ" on his next production. Though noted film composer Stanley Myers was already working on the soundtrack, Matthew Fisher was called upon to contribute as well.

Fisher met up with Bond and played him different Procol Harum songs. They both agreed it would be a good idea to use the Brooker-Reid song "Salad Days (Are Here Again)" for the film, and Matthew Fisher also finished off an instrumental theme which he had already been working on for a few weeks. This track eventually took its name from the title of the film.

Based on both ascending and descending bass lines, diminished chords and an abundance of tricks from the book of chorale harmonisation, "Separation" is an outstandingly coherent and impressive piece of music written by the twenty-one year old Fisher, who around the same time, according to a press release, was also starting work on a solo album. Unfortunately, this album never got off the ground, a fate shared by several other planned Procol Harum-related projects during 1967, including starring roles in *Seventeen Plus*, a film about "a pop group which becomes more powerful than the Government as a result of teenagers being given voting powers" (*NME*, 23.9.67).

Separation was shown only briefly at cinemas in London. It used a rather chopped-up edit of "Salad Days", while the instrumental title track had been recorded with Matthew Fisher on Hammond organ, Stanley Myers on harpsichord and Cliff Barton (formerly with Georgie Fame) playing bass guitar. In 1973 a longer version of the track, augmented with a string arrangement, appeared on Fisher's first solo album, *Journey's End*.

The original film soundtrack also featured several other themes, some of them written by Stanley Myers and involving Matthew Fisher playing his trusted M102. Unfortunately, none of this music has ever been released on record.

It isn't just the combination of a truly excellent, frightfully young lyric writer and a highly original composer that makes for the immense artistic success of the first Procol Harum album. Rather this achievement is based on the contributions of everyone involved, and it is interesting to observe how each player in the group managed to reflect, in his own musical interpretations, separate aspects enclosed in Reid's lyrics.

I have alluded to Gary Brooker's singing as sounding "matter-of-fact". As a private person he is renowned for his relaxed, dead-pan manner, which is something journalists picked up on right from the start. Such an attitude is perfect for singing rhythm 'n' blues, a style that often calls on a somewhat dry and wry delivery. Apart from being the group's main songwriter Brooker also contributed these particular qualities to Procol Harum via his magnificent voice, and in doing so he enhanced some important aspects of Reid's lyrics – the irony, the humour, the almost demonic "cool".

However, the desperate sense of futility which is another major feature in Reid's writing, the notion of being tossed around like a ship on a stormy sea, is primarily reflected in Matthew Fisher's playing. There seems to be a strange triangle formed by Reid's lyrics, the sound of the Hammond, and Matthew Fisher's way of playing it – the long-drawn notes, the eminent use of both manuals, the extreme skill and awe-inspiring attention to detail.

The remaining lyrical aspects – the physical intensity, the sensual yearnings – are left to Robin Trower to communicate. It sounds a horrible cliché, but his playing almost makes the guitar "speak". I have this zany notion that were anyone to analyze human speech in all its aspects – frequencies, harmonics, articulation – and compare it to Trower's playing, they might find the results to be not that far apart. You can put it down to things like sound and phrasing, but in reality it's not technically founded at all – it all comes down to musical instinct.

We find the heavyweight duo of Barrie James Wilson and David Knights not driving this volcano of artistic energy as much as forming a solid basis beneath it, a plinth. Since the early Paramounts days BJ Wilson had steadily developed into an unusual, highly creative drummer. Extremely dynamic, humorous and original he is quite simply one of the greatest percussionists of rock 'n' roll. Right from the start he was a strong catalyst in shaping Procol Harum's overall musical image.

Perhaps he and Knights were uneven partners in the sense that Wilson was immensely technically articulate and Dave Knights was a much more straightforward player. But all ships need an anchor, and in taking that role on the Harum ship Knights was no less of a force than anyone else. Apparently he would often receive clear instructions from Brooker about what to play, but even when he evidently starts to go his own way his bass lines are still pretty similar to what you would normally think up on a piano. Perhaps you could say that Knights is a bass player with the ability to "think like the lower end of a piano" – in other words a natural choice for a two-keyboard line-up.

Not long after having finished work their first LP the group recorded two new tracks, "Seem To Have The Blues (Most All Of The Time)" and "Monsieur Armand". Surprisingly, these songs are closer to a straightforward blues format than anything The Paramounts ever released, both tracks featuring some impressive guitar. Likewise Fisher's Hammond work is splendid and indicative of the kind of style he had been playing in different groups until now.

Both lyrics could be described as self-mocking existentialist blues with a good deal of humour thrown in. "Monsieur Armand" seems to partly draw on the old "Dr Jekyll and Mr Hyde" theme but could in fact just as easily be a storyline for an episode of the famous 1980s BBC comedy series *The Young Ones*. "Seem To Have The Blues" is the first of a small group of Reid lyrics where the narrator happens to be a deceased person.

The rhythm section's performance on both recordings is acceptable, though it can't be denied that the songs seem to yell out in vain for a bit of "funk" or "groove". More importantly the lead vocals are not entirely up to Brooker's normal standard, which could explain why none of the tracks was released at the time (they didn't appear until 1976 on the Decca compilation series *Rock Roots*).

To improve the group's visual image, the services of Dutch design-er-couple Seemon & Marijke, who had previously been working for The Beatles, were called upon. It didn't take them long to fashion and create a set of wonderful, psychedelic suits for the members of Procol Harum.

Dave Knights remembers: "My outfit consisted of a pair of brilliant red vinyl boots going up to the knee with criss-cross lacing all the way down (very kinky), a pair of velvet, mauve, purple trousers, and tucked into these a gold silk blouse. God, I lost a lot of friends over this! Gary had a blue cloak with a skull-cap which had a star on it. Fisher was all dressed in green. Later on, when we were playing in Paris, I think he found that it made it impossible for him to catch a cab...

"We went home, tried them all on – and I could not walk in these boots. Couldn't walk in them. They really hurt. And we went back. We had to dress up in all these things again... He said, 'Oh, and by the way it's £200 an outfit.' Back in 1967, £200 was a lot of money.

"Immediately after we went to France to play an open air festival. Every band that went on before us was pelted with tomatoes. The whole stage was slippery with tomatoes, and we came on in these clothes. Nobody pelted, thank God, and we played – and the news the next day was, *The tomato psychedelic group!*"

By all accounts Procol Harum actually wore these outfits – chris-tened "the Medieval Spacemen Suits" by Gary Brooker – for a few months, then one by one they found they'd had enough and threw them away. Most of the clothes were collected by Brooker, who could still be seen wearing bits and pieces of them several years later.

Shipped across the sea

No psychedelic thing goes on; instead they play beautiful tunes some-where in between the music of Bach, soul and modern jazz. Slowly it moves deep into your body and at the end of the concert you have dreamt yourself far away.

Sven Wezelenburg (*New Musical Express*, 9.9.67)

While a lot of things went wrong for Procol Harum in their homeland during the early days of their career, America still represented a fresh territory. "A Whiter Shade Of Pale" had gone to Number 5 in the charts there, which may not sound overwhelmingly impressive con-sidering its success elsewhere. Nevertheless, it is characteristic of Procol Harum that it wasn't really a question of creating immediate and short-lived chart-stormering success. The kind of hits they had were more consistent, a point proven by the fact that over the last thir-ty years the band's first four LPs have rarely been unavailable. Keith Reid:

"After the first album we went to America. We didn't think we had any kind of career in the rest of the world at all. So that's why people knew a lot more about us in America, 'cause we toured there a lot. People in England – all they ever heard was 'A Whiter Shade Of Pale' and 'Homburg'."

Many explanations could be given for the band's almost permanent residence in the States between 1967 and 1971, a lot of them practical.

One important reason for their popularity and high overseas sales figures was quite simply that the US release of *Procol Harum* included "A Whiter Shade Of Pale".

This was possible because the release of the album came early in the US, in September 1967. At this point New Breed Productions were still working under some kind of contract with Deram/Decca. However, in the UK things got held up, meaning that the contract ran out and suddenly Denny Cordell found himself trying to strike a new deal with another label – a process which delayed things even further.

Eventually he ended up signing to Regal Zonophone, who until then had mainly been EMI's outlet for Salvation Army records (their one and only chart entry so far being the Joy Strings' "It's An Open Secret" from 1964). In America the new deal was with A&M, in Germany it was with Polydor – all pretty confusing and adding to the chaos.

Owing to the change of record label the release of *Procol Harum* in the UK could not automatically include the all-important hit. Perhaps some kind of leasing arrangement ought to have been embarked upon, but it didn't happen.

Procol Harum wasn't released in Britain until January 1968. By then the group had practically lost all the momentum of their initial successes, and the public and press had long since written them off as two-hit-wonders, a ridiculous status they seem to have maintained up until this very day. Robin Trower:

"My situation was... well, when a group's Number 1 you don't turn it down, it's just too good an opportunity to miss. I found a lot of the material interesting, they were all very good musicians, they had BJ on drums... But we always worked under the feeling of it being a real struggle... They [the early group] didn't grasp the opportunity when it came along and, of course, once it had gone it dissipates very quickly. Consequently you're always trying to claw your way back up, and I think it's easier to have *not* made it and try to work your way up than having made it and fallen and trying to claw your way back up. I think that's almost a Herculean task. And, of course, to work under that pressure all the time of having to follow the biggest Number 1 record of the year, it's just – forget it!"

The story of early Procol Harum on tour is about as baffling and seemingly self-destructive as the rest of their career at this point. In

Above left: The Society Five circa 1963, featuring Matthew Fisher on bass. The guitarist on the left is Mike Roberts, 35 years later, the winner of the British Songwriter Competition. *Photo: unknown*
Above right: Richard Brown, Procol Harum's first guitarist. *Photo: Ken Jensen*
Below: The Paramounts in 1965 - If everything else failed there was always the ice cream van. (l-r) BJ Wilson, Robin Trower, Diz Derrick and (lying down) Gary Brooker. *Photo: © EMI Records UK*

Above: Gary Brooker and the Medieval Spacemen, 1967. (clockwise) Gary Brooker, Dave Knights, Robin Trower, BJ Wilson and Matthew Fisher. *Photo: unknown*

Left and above:
On stage at Falkoner Centret, Copenhagen, 1967.

(l-r) Gary Brooker, Dave Knights, Robin Trower and Matthew Fisher.
Photos: Jan Persson.

Above: Keith Reid in Scandinavia, October 1967. *Photo: Jan Persson*
Below : Late 1969 rehearsals in the country for the *Home* album,
with Chris Copping back in the fold (bottom right). *Photos: Robin Copping*

Top: (l-r) Three Procols playing it cool. (l-r) Robin Trower, BJ Wilson and Chris Copping.
Photo: Robin Copping

Middle: Back on stage in Copenhagen, 1971 (l-r) Gary Brooker, BJ Wilson and Chris Copping.
Photo: Jan Persson.

Bottom: Gary Brooker ponders over one of Keith Reid's lyrics. Copenhagen 1971.
Photo: Jan Persson.

Recording for Danish State TV, October 1974.
Top left: Mick Grabham shows Alan Cartwright the way to the men's room. **Top right:** BJ Wilson.
Bottom: Gary Brooker with tissues - Scandinavian tours usually meant catching a cold. *Photos: Jan Persson.*

Above: Hero Bob Dylan looks down on Keith Reid.
Photo: Peder Bundgaard.

Left: Gary Brooker with a souvenir from London - a banjo.
Photo: Peder Bundgaard.

Opposite top: Gary Brooker in a reflective mood, 1990.
Photo: Nik Kalinowski

Opposite bottom: Four to the bar - Procol in Paris, 1992, fronted by Gary Brooker. Behind him are Dave Bronze, Matthew Fisher and Mark Brzezicki. In the background, newcomer Geoff Whitehorn waits for permission to join.
Photo: Nik Kalinowski

Left: Citizen Brooker and cohorts take over Paris
Paris, 1992.
Above: Geoff Whitehorn.
Below: On stage in Tallinn, Estonia, July 1993.
(l-r) Geoff Whitehorn, Dave Bronze, Gary Brooker,
Matthew Fisher and Ian Wallace,
Photos: Nik Kalinowski

the earliest days, when Harrison and Royer were in the line-up and "A Whiter Shade Of Pale" was at its chart peak, the group had played a string of generally low-paid gigs in smaller club venues around the UK.

Matthew Fisher remembered that, "The impression I got was that as soon as the record had crept into the lower part of the charts our manager at the time had gone over to the agency who were handling the bookings for him and said, 'Yeah, yeah, record's in the charts, book 'em up, book 'em up.' So they just booked about six months to a year of solid work, all for about £50-£60 a night, quite shitty venues, nothing at all prestigious, very low money – rather than waiting to see what the record did, you know, waiting another week or two to see if it was gonna go up or come down again, or whatever. So that was it, by the time we were Number 1 we were travelling around with a band that really weren't terribly good, playing some very bad gigs for very low money. The promoters must have been laughing themselves silly, 'cause when they booked the band they just thought they were getting another band. Then it turns out, by the time that the gig comes around, it's the group that happens to be Number 1 in the charts at the time, and all for £50-£60."

Fisher's statement can be supported by taking a quick glance at the group's touring schedule for mid-June 1967, which included Sheffield's Mojo, York's Tinned Chicken, Downham's Bal Tabarin, Tavistock Town Hall and so on. Probably all cosy enough little places to go and hear a local band, but rather low-profile gigs for a group having Decca's fastest-selling single ever and a major world-wide Number 1 hit. No wonder Denny Cordell suddenly cancelled the tour, pulled the band off the road and took them into the recording studio instead.

After the arrival of Trower and Wilson the group immediately went off to places like Belgium and Scandinavia, where they went down a storm. "We had to play some dates abroad to get ourselves together," David Knights admitted. No sooner had they returned to Britain, they set off on their first American tour. No wonder UK fans felt let down.

In the US Procol Harum performed a full week at The Fillmore in San Francisco. After that they appeared at The Winterland along with Pink Floyd and The Doors.

Over the next two and a half years they would do no fewer than nine major tours of the States. Dave Knights:

"After a few tours in Europe and in the States – I would say about the third tour of the States – we started to become a 'live' band that was delivering on stage. We worked up very slowly by supporting different people, and then we started to headline... I was into playing 'live' more than recording and it was very much an education to play in the States, to be on bills with people who were legends. There was a lot of excitement in the air, everything was new. We were young and green, very much so...

"I remember playing at The Winterland in San Francisco, where we supported The Doors. I came off stage and there were these sort of beautiful hippie-type ladies saying, 'Wow, you're amazing, what sign are you?' They thought we were into all sorts of drugs – and my biggest crime was drinking pints of bitter, or lager in the States. We were very straight, really. It was just that the music led people to believe we were on something and they wanted to find out what it was. We weren't at all. I never even took an aspirin, still don't. I was very against doing anything like that. Not for any moral reasons, it was just that I didn't like to put those kinds of things in my body."

Knights' statement here has been somewhat contradicted by other group members over the years. Talking to former *Melody Maker* editor Chris Welch in connection with the 1997 Repertoire CD release of *Shine On Brightly*, Keith Reid commented on the title track:

"There were probably some psychedelic drugs involved in that one. It was very hard to avoid that in America at the time. I was there – like everybody else."

Likewise Gary Brooker has admitted to taking "pills" and smoking hash, at least during The Paramounts days (the booklet for Castle's CD release of *Procol's Ninth* shows a picture of him smoking something that doesn't quite look like a normal home-rolled cigarette to me; Keith Reid is grinning in the background). Matthew Fisher has already commented elsewhere on the consequences of smoking hash and furthermore told me, "BJ did everything excessively, including drugs".

However, it must be said that I have found no evidence of Robin Trower and David Knights being anything other than completely straight. Furthermore, it doesn't appear that hard drugs or severe drug abuse were ever a dominant feature in the history of Procol Harum, and unlike some of their audience I fail to find many drug references in their lyrics. As Keith Reid put it: "If I took drugs and based my lyrics on that... I always felt it would be like cheating."

With touring inevitably came a lot of involvement with the press. After having listened to and read countless interviews with the group over the years I can only describe them as pretty inconsistent. Sometimes it would go well, particularly if the person conducting the interview was more of a fan than a journalist. At other times you wonder why the band even bothered to confront the press.

A good example is Neil Drummond's article in *New Musical Express*, October 1967, which starts: "There are times in everyone's lives when one feels it would be much nicer to be somewhere else." Apparently none of Drummond's questions had been answered with more than three words. It is perhaps worth mentioning that at this point the *New Musical Express* had been writing about Procol Harum every single week for four months, praising their music and their personalities and practically never printing a single word that in any way compromised the group.

In somewhat the same manner Keith Reid would always be very elusive when questioned about his lyrics.

"Keith was a very unusual character," Dave Knights said. "I think he created a mystique. He didn't talk to people unless he wanted to talk to people. If he found them boring he would just look at them. He used to terrify some people and not others. Looking back on it I think he was probably quite shy."

Perhaps Reid himself cut closer to the bone in the Chris Welch interview for Repertoire Records, where he stated, "I'm more secure and more confident in my ability now."

It was particularly important to ask Reid about his lyrics because the group's records generally didn't include lyric sheets. Two songs were printed on the sleeve of *Shine On Brightly*, while *Home* and *Broken Barricades* included six and four lyrics respectively. The UK edition of 1973's *Grand Hotel* had a limited edition lyric booklet. Apart from that it wasn't until 1975, with the release of *Procol's Ninth*, that a Harum LP had a full lyric sheet.

Adding to the confusion was Gary Brooker's use of his voice primarily as a lead instrument, with diction taking a back seat. To sum up the situation, few people outside the group had much chance of understanding what Keith Reid's lyrics were all about.

Books could be written of how fans over the years have misheard Procol Harum lyrics. In a way, such books exist – Procol Harum bootleg lyric books – which suggests that there were interested and keen followers out there who were perhaps not being rewarded properly for their enthusiasm.

I recall presenting Matthew Fisher with such a publication and suggesting he and I work our way through it together, correcting all the mistakes. After all, I imagined it would be an easier process than writing down all the lyrics from start to finish. As always Matthew was extremely helpful, and his memory in this area was almost uncannily clear.

Halfway through, Fisher's then-wife Linda kindly brought us each a cup of tea. She cast a glance at what we were doing and immediately burst out laughing. I explained to her that in fact this was one of the better examples of what fans thought Keith Reid's lyrics were. Leaving the room she gazed briefly at her husband and muttered, "No wonder they thought you were a weird group."

With such a basis for misinterpretation it's not surprising that Keith Reid's writings were often perceived as impenetrable. In some interviews he seems astonished when journalists ask him about lyrics which to him obviously are rather straightforward - and probably would have been to the journalists as well, had they had a chance to see them on paper.

Luckily, the situation is much better today, with the majority of Reid's lyrics being available in correct form on the Procol Harum Internet Website, *Beyond The Pale*. Furthermore there has for some time been talk of a limited edition publication gathering them all under one umbrella.

Since Brooker-Reid were the main writers, most interviews would naturally be centred on them. Apart from very early on, Matthew Fisher and David Knights would rarely step forward. The fact that Fisher only gradually became part of the songwriting team, and that he and Knights had never been in The Paramounts, seems to have made them feel a bit isolated at times. On top of that it is no secret that some members found Matthew Fisher difficult to get along with.

"We would always put Dave up with Matthew when we were on tour," Keith Reid told me. "Dave is such a nice person, so resourceful."

Dave Knights recalls: "When Matthew went to bed I used to creep out and go down different clubs with BJ and we used to down an awful lot of beers, meet up with different people, just have fun. Then I'd stagger back to the hotel. Matthew always used to throw shoes at me, saying, 'Be quiet. I'm trying to sleep!'"

According to Gary Brooker, Fisher didn't like to go on tour. "He would rather be at home with his mum, I think, sleep until six, get up and play a little and then go back to bed again."

All the other members appear to have had the exact opposite attitude.

"Quite frankly," Dave Knights told me. "When I was on the road somewhere like in the States, if someone had said, 'You can't ever go home, you gotta stay here,' I would have been perfectly happy. I could adapt, but Matthew wanted to go home. I always remember Robin, in fact, being 'British'. He brought his own teapot and tea, because 'you couldn't get a good cup of tea in the States.'"

Travelling and touring also meant striking up friendships with other musicians.

"We got to know The Band very well," Keith Reid recalled, "because we used to go and stay in Woodstock a lot. What really happened was a drag. The notes on the sleeve of *Shine On Brightly* were written by Paul Williams who had also made a great review of the first album. He made some comment about The Band and for sure Robbie Robertson was really pissed off about it. But it was nothing to do with us. Still, Robbie Robertson made some negative remarks about us, I think because of that. It was a real shame. But we used to know that group Mountain quite well and their drummer was from Canada, and he told us that The Band had heard us and they'd listened to us quite a lot. I know Bob Dylan had listened to us. The similarity however between us and The Band had probably more to do with being influenced by the same kind of music. Then we got very friendly with them, we made tapes with them, playing with them and everything. I don't think we got to know Robbie Robertson, but Levon and Garth and all the others." (Unfortunately, it hasn't been possible to trace these tapes, and other group members don't recall making them.

Perhaps Reid confuses the situation with some recordings Procol Harum made around the same time at a studio belonging to the band Mountain – more of that later.)

The lack of visual image, of a stage show, or even just an elaborate light show, arguably added to the general problems with keeping up the high level of initial success.

"Basically the band stood there and played the songs," Keith Reid told Chris Welch. "People appreciated it but, in retrospect, it was a shame we didn't have a big light show. Nobody in the band was really into all that, so it didn't happen."

Yet another important aspect of touring was performing on television and radio shows. Procol Harum's first ever "live" appearance with the Trower-Wilson line-up was a television show in Belgium, and over the following years they would frequently perform on such shows in the US and on mainland Europe.

In Britain they only appeared on a few television shows during the very early stage of their career, but throughout the sixties they would often play sessions for BBC's *Top of the Pops* radio show, whose chief disc jockey was Brian Matthews. Listening back to these shows today - which on the whole feature excellent performances – it is obvious that Matthews was fond of the band, which is probably why he kept asking them to come back. Apart from their normal repertoire the group recorded for the BBC a version of Tim Rose's "Morning Dew", a song they had also performed with Jimi Hendrix on stage at the Speakeasy Club in 1967.

While on the subject of covering other people's material it should be mentioned that around the same time the group also performed as part of their "live" act a song called "Dirty Water" (a 1966 garage-rock hit for The Standells, and a UK hit for The Inmates in 1979), Richard Strauss' "Also Sprach Zarathustra" (also known as "The Theme From 2001"), and a straightforward blues song titled "Going Down Slow". Audience bootleg recordings of some of these songs exist, but no official versions.

Finally, during one of their American tours the band recorded four tracks at a studio belonging to the group Mountain. These recordings were made only for fun and featured the members of Procol Harum swapping instruments and taking turns at singing. A four track 7" acetate from this session still exists and includes not particularly wonderful versions of "Twist And Shout" (sung by Robin Trower), "It's So Easy" (sung by Dave Knights with Matthew Fisher on lead guitar), "I've Gotta Get A Message To You" (a duet between Knights and Fisher) and – the best of the bunch – "Keep A-Knocking" (sung by Gary Brooker).

Quite rightly so

> They're still one of my all-time favourite bands. I have all their albums, and they're all brilliant. But my favourite will always be *Shine On Brightly*. That is quite simply a fantastic LP.
>
> A fan (at Exeter Record Fair, January 1999)

Something was brewing underneath the psychedelic rock scene in England as 1967 turned into 1968. Over the following year groups who had previously been singles-orientated suddenly started to release LP records which included long, epic works. Mod heroes The Small Faces exchanged their fish-tail parkas for multi-coloured boiler suits and set about recording the whimsical, vaudeville-inspired *Ogden's Nut Gone Flake*, while R&B workmen The Pretty Things came up with the sombre *S.F. Sorrow*. These were fine albums, but it wasn't really until 1969, when The Who's *Tommy* came out, that the world finally took to the idea of the concept album.

Since the autumn of 1967 Keith Reid had been playing with the thought of joining the songs on side two of the next Procol Harum LP into some kind of a unity. The initial inspiration may have been The Beatles' *Sgt. Pepper* album, but in other ways the music of Procol Harum was a far cry from the Liverpool four's all-time classic.

Initially, Harum seem to have been intended as a British parallel to what Bob Dylan was doing at the time. They had, however, soon developed their own unique style which defied categorisation. Too serious to be a pop band, too ethereal to be political, too sombre to be psychedelic, too R&B orientated to be progressive, you either concluded that this group were sitting between too many stools or you saw them as kings of their own wonderful self-made niche.

Still Procol Harum were very much part of a world where popular music was undergoing serious changes, some of which they were obviously affected by. Their second LP, *Shine On Brightly*, was not conceived in a vacuum.

It came to life in a short period between late 1967 and early 1968 during gaps in the group's touring schedule, meaning that work on the record had already started before the first album was released in the UK.

Lyrically it elaborates on the themes embarked upon on the first LP, particularly those belonging in what we have established as "category two". Track-by-track analysis is hardly necessary – in nearly every song on this album the narrator complains about his inability to find some deeper philosophical/religious meaning in life.

There are several indications that he has at a point experienced some kind of a "glimpse" – a minor form of revelation. This theme was already present in "Kaleidoscope" on the first LP, and we find it mentioned again on this album in songs like "Wish Me Well", "Rambling On" and "Glimpses Of Nirvana".

If the overall mood is in any way different from before, it is darker, more engulfed in self-despair and gloom garnished with the narrator's declarations of his own insanity. The "sin", which he repeatedly mentions, seems not to be traditionally Old Testament-like as much as the crime of wasting one's life, perhaps by searching self-indulgently for some overall truth which is beyond the grasp of the narrator.

Some followers of the group would spend a considerable time wondering what Reid meant by letting the Dalai Lama in "Glimpses Of Nirvana" compare life with a beanstalk, for instance. However, the notion that Keith Reid should possess some kind of deeper understanding of human existence which he wants his audience to seek out by interpretation is contradicted by the entire record stating the opposite. Really, these songs are about the desperation of having nothing to report.

It is only when the words are set to music that a more profound dimension emerges. This particularly goes for the long joined-up track on side two, "In Held 'Twas In I" which, via the musical contributions of Brooker and Fisher, is shaped into a modern apocalypse. This is indicated by the threatening drone at the opening of the first track and Brooker's terse rendition of the text, through the escalating, menacing chaos of "In The Autumn Of My Madness" (featuring more Bach-esque modulations than even Victor Borge ever managed), to the eventual harmony and revelation reflected in the choral beauty of "Grand Finale".

A modern apocalypse is an incredibly ambitious framework for any artist to employ. Procol Harum not only got away with it phenomenally well, they also later in their career embarked twice on similar projects with "Whaling Stories" (1970) and – albeit less convincingly – "The Worm And The Tree" (1977).

Perhaps the songs on *Shine On Brightly* more than elsewhere underline why Reid is primarily a lyric writer, not a poet. On their own these words (as he himself insisted on calling his lyrics) seem somewhat incomplete. That is not a drawback – on the contrary it is a quality. They are yelling out to be supplemented by music, which is their very purpose.

It isn't the existentialist subject matter that makes Reid lyrics unique for their time, nor their use of imagery, nor their anachronistic vocabulary. What singles them out is the fact that he manages to incorporate it all into a traditional pop song format, with rhymes, rigid structures, sometimes even choruses – while still leaving room for something extra to be added in the form of music.

Shine On Brightly was released in two very different sleeves. The UK version had a mock-Surrealist painting by George Underwood using the morbid imagery of Keith Reid's lyrics, relating primarily the title track. The main object is a pink and light-blue grand piano with its lid open, a clock with frog's legs standing on it and a row of zombies inside, the back end of the instrument running infinitely out towards the horizon.

The back of the sleeve has Paul Williams' sleeve-notes at the top with the lyrics for "Quite Rightly So" and "Magdalene (My Regal Zonophone)" printed underneath. On the bottom half is the track-listing itemising the different songs included in "In Held 'Twas In I".The US sleeve only stated the overall title. However, that is a small difference compared with the fact that it featured an altogether different illustration. Not a painting, but a strangely greenish photograph of a vandalised upright piano and a female shop-mannequin standing on a sea bed. The back of the sleeve has a close-up photo of the same piano with a broken toy motorcyclist placed on the ledge above the keys.

The US sleeve is a "gatefold", its inside showing a murky mono-chrome photo of the group, Gary Brooker and BJ Wilson each holding a sparkler (incidentally, the other members also held sparklers but those two are the only ones you can see). Underneath are the sleeve-notes, containing the same two lyrics as on the British version, a more rudimentary track-listing together with a small photograph of the same upright piano, this time with the dummy lying awkwardly across the keys. The photographs are by Guy Webster, the art director is Tom Wilkes.

It seems that while George Underwood's painting takes Reid's lyrics at face value, Tom Wilkes goes further and makes a more per-sonal analysis. The dreamy, unreal quality of the photographs used in his artwork isn't far removed from the feeling you get when you listen to the album. The rigidity and tattiness of the mannequin along with the broken toy seem to suggest that some kind of rough treatment could be involved in causing the unhappiness displayed in the lyrical content. Both the mannequin and the motorcyclist have lost their arms. Adding to this theme of amputation one of the bottom keys on the piano is missing, a feature emphasised by the close-up photo on the back of the sleeve.

Is has been suggested that the reason for the different sleeves was that Procol Harum's American label (A&M) refused to use George Underwood's painting, because they found it offensive. I fail to see what could have caused such a judgement.

Perhaps someone got the story the wrong way around. It is more probable that Regal Zonophone – a former Salvation Army Label – would have deemed the US sleeve offensive with its naked, amputat-ed mannequin. Furthermore, the record was released in the US no fewer than three months before it became available to British buyers. Incidentally, the German pressing on Polydor (released in November 1968) used the American design but was a single-sleeve.

The UK edition was not unique just for its sleeve but also for appearing both in a mono and a stereo mix (elsewhere it came out in stereo only). This is the only Procol Harum album to have received such a treatment. It may be relevant to mention that the making of both such mixes was common in the UK between the early sixties and 1970.

The stereo mix of *Shine On Brightly* was extremely well balanced for its time, but something must have happened at the pressing plant which cut away a substantial part of the low end frequencies on the album. The mono mix is better in this area. Furthermore, it has that robust, integrated feel you always get with mono and which many collectors and audiophiles tend to prefer.

In the case of this particular record, the original UK mono version (issued only on vinyl), and the current stereo compact disc release by German label Repertoire (featuring the US sleeve) are recommended. This edition has more "punch" than the UK release by Westside. However, the Westside CD includes several interesting unreleased recordings, among these the legendary "Alpha" with Bill Eyden on drums, recorded on the same day as "A Whiter Shade Of Pale". In fact, serious collectors need all three issues, plus possibly the original US edition for its impressive "gatefold" sleeve.

Like its predecessor *Shine On Brightly* was recorded at Advision Studios and Olympic I and II, though this time a few tracks were also done at De Lane Lea. Most of the time the band were working at Olympic II, which was Denny Cordell's favourite studio. "'Twas Teatime At The Circus" was recorded at De Lane Lea, and the chorus for "Grand Finale" had to be done at Advision Studios, which apparently was the only studio in Britain at the time to have eight-track facilities.

On all the other songs two four-track machines were used. The technique employed at the time was to use up all four tracks on one recorder, and then mix them down to two tracks on the other four-track machine. That left two extra tracks to record on, and theoretically the process could be continued *ad infinitum* = or rather until the tape noise became unbearable. Also the "mix-down-as-you-go-along" procedure obviously limited the engineer's control over the final mix.

This technique – known as "four-to-four" – had been utilised abundantly by The Beatles on *Sgt. Pepper*. Procol Harum's first album had mostly been recorded straight on to four tracks, with the occasional vocal, piano or guitar part overdubbed. On *Shine On Brightly*, however, a lot of then-state-of-the-art technique was employed. Studio engineers were Glyn Johns, Eddie Kramer and Alan O'Duffy. Officially, Denny Cordell was still the band's producer.

"Tony Visconti did quite a lot of work on it," recalled Keith Reid. "As far as 'In Held 'Twas In I' goes we did it all in pieces, and Glyn Johns made it sound as a whole. He engineered quite a lot of that album and he did a great job. Denny Cordell never had any input into the group at all."

Musically Procol Harum had changed a lot since their first, mainly R&B influenced album. The classical inspirations were stronger now. There is only one song on the album – "Wish Me Well" – which is fundamentally a blues track. Elsewhere baroque chord sequences reign in more or less mutated forms, with melody taking a back seat.

In fact, the absence of ear-catching, romantic melody lines (in Brooker's compositions, not in Matthew Fisher's) is one of the main areas where Procol Harum were distinctively un-British. Popular music in Britain has always been melodically based, but Gary Brooker's way of constructing a melody line has more in common with what the lead instrument in a Bach piece is doing, where a typical feature is the repetition of brief melodic sequences in different positions on top of changing chord structures.

On paper this method of writing looks mechanical; performed in the right manner, however, the result can be an almost metaphysical experience (which was undoubtedly what Bach was aiming at). It is an unusual way to write for a rock group and so closely suited to Brooker's voice and singing style that I doubt anyone else could ever get away with performing the majority of his songs.

The *Shine On Brightly* LP is also significant for giving more space to Matthew Fisher both as composer and singer. By his own account, Fisher wrote the chord sequence for the opening track, "Quite Rightly So", while Brooker composed the melody to go along with it. Fisher also co-wrote the entire song cycle "In Held 'Twas In I" with Brooker, performed the lead vocal on "In The Autumn Of My Madness", and played acoustic rhythm guitar on several tracks ("Quite Rightly So", "Rambling On", "In The Autumn Of My Madness"). Finally, Fisher played harpsichord on "Look To Your Soul" and "'Twas Tea Time At The Circus", as well as glockenspiel on the latter.

Most of side one sees Gary Brooker giving a string of superb examples of how to interpret song lyrics musically, to the point where we are even invited on a trip down to Hell. This happens in "Skip Softly (My Moonbeams)" where, unsurprisingly, the journey goes via a long descending bass line ending in a sea of drones and Spanish inspired piano phrases. Then follows a sharp, distorted guitar solo churning like a knife inside a wound, and finally a manic sabre dance lifted from Katchachurian, which seems to tumble down endlessly into a maelstrom of sound.

Brooker's voice soars over most of the LP, stronger than ever, clearly matured since the first album, and always a miracle of precision and musicality. It seems to peak on "Look To Your Soul", his best vocal effort up to this point (though soon overtaken by his performance on "A Salty Dog"). The piano playing is less prominent than in The Paramounts' days but still an important part of the soundscape, eagerly collaborating with Fisher's Hammond, forming exciting and surprising little figures underneath the voice, the words, and the solos.

The album also shows Procol Harum growing more into a real band, a musically integrated group of people, each with unique talents and an urgency to express themselves. On the two opening tracks, which are quite similar in style and structure, Fisher's Hammond playing is taken to a new extreme. Over previously established chord sequences he builds magnificent little themes, small masterworks of taste and timing.

BJ Wilson on this record quite simply invents the style for which he would later became so renowned – the start/stop technique, the constant creative unpredictability. David Knights adds not only weight but also some fine, soul-inspired lines, particularly on the first two songs.

Robin Trower's playing is worth a study on its own as he continually manages somehow to find unorthodox things to say, keeping within his blues framework no matter what everyone else might be doing. His rhythm playing (if such a term is appropriate) on "Rambling On" is simply astonishing. I think he is a better vocalist than he displays on the duet with Brooker on "Wish Me Well", but the song features some stunning solo guitar. At this point Trower was not yet technically the guitar hero he would later become, but the feel is tremendous.

The long track on side two is where the group really start to cut loose.

"Matthew got very frustrated after the first album," recalled Keith Reid. "We wanted to involve him more in the songwriting. One of the reasons for doing that long track was that it was something he could get involved with. It was not a concept album, but it was a conscious thing to do this very long track.

"It sort of wrote itself. We just started off, and at that time we never had any idea that it was going to be as long as it turned out, but we just kept adding bits on and on. There was no conscious continuity, but when it was all put together it seemed to be there anyhow."

Even the itemised breakdown of "In Held 'Twas In I" featured on the British edition of the album seems to me inadequate. Here is a more detailed attempt:

"In Held 'Twas In I"

I. "Glimpses Of Nirvana"
- a) First spoken lyric (Gary Brooker + drone)
- b) Instrumental No. 1 (band - piano)
- c) Instrumental No. 2 (sitar theme, repeated with voices)
- d) Second spoken lyric (Keith Reid + piano)

II. "'Twas Tea Time A The Circus" (Gary Brooker, vocal)

III. "In The Autumn Of My Madness"
- a) Main song (Matthew Fisher, vocal)
- b) Instrumental No. 3 (atonal guitar/bass/organ riff)
- c) Instrumental No. 2 revisited (electric guitar)

IV "Look To Your Soul" (Gary Brooker, vocal)

V. "Grand Finale" (band + choir)

According to Keith Reid, Fisher wrote the music for two of the tracks, "In The Autumn Of My Madness" and "Grand Finale". Gary Brooker wrote "'Twas Teatime At The Circus" and "Look To Your Soul".

Matthew Fisher further told me that what is listed here as "First spoken lyric" had music by Gary Brooker. He also wrote "Instrumental No. 2" (the sitar theme), while "Instrumental No. 1" (the chromatic, rising theme ending in a series of Tchaikovsky-esque piano chords) was written by Fisher himself who has always referred to it as "Rude Awakening".

The music for "Second spoken lyric", the slow piano piece over which Keith Reid recites, was Brooker's work, though the idea of introducing a clock chime, which in fact is played on a tubular bell, was an idea Matthew Fisher had picked up from Tchaikovsky's *Hamlet Overture*. Fisher also recalled writing the scale leading up to the chorus of "'Twas Tea Time At The Circus" as well as the chorus itself; the rest of the song was, as already mentioned, written by Brooker. Finally Matthew Fisher remembered contributing the first set of variant chords used on "Instrumental No. 2 revisited", probably with Brooker writing the bass line.

On "Glimpses Of Nirvana" Brooker played a koto (a Japanese string instrument), and the sitar theme was played by a female Indian player, whose name everyone now unfortunately seems to have forgotten. On "Grand Finale" a choir of friends, roadies and studio crew was employed, with female voices supplied by Gary Brooker's wife Franky, and Robin Trower's fiancé (later wife) Andrea.

"I nicked the theme for that from Haydn," Fisher admitted. "But there were problems with the guitar solo. We knew that Rob's solos seemed to work best in minor key chord sequences. Major chord sequences didn't really go with the blues scale he was playing with. Actually the chords we ended up using were taken from the theme Gary had written earlier on and used underneath Keith's reciting his own lyrics ['Second spoken lyric']. We thought, 'Right, okay, we take that, transpose it into some suitable key and – off you go, Rob!'"

The unusual title simply came from taking the first word in each of the songs and putting them together. Literally it has little meaning, but a number of suitable connotations can be inferred: "In Hell Was I", "Hell Was In I", "Held Was I" and so on.

None of it particularly uplifting stuff. Nevertheless, the uplifting element is there. It lies in the fact that out of all this "gloom and doom" evolves something artistically interesting. Intelligent and uncompromising, the music of Procol Harum didn't exactly promote the comfortable life ethos of "taking the bad with the good". What they did instead was take the bad and turn it into something that was very good indeed.

Shine On Brightly influenced a lot of other artists, some of them considerably more commercially successful than Procol Harum at the time. You seem to find traces of the album in both the music of The Who, Billy Joel, Little Feat and many others.

It's difficult to judge whether it influenced The Beatles as well, since they in fact had invented the "semi-concept formula" a year before Procol Harum utilised it. But it is remarkable that side two of the *Abbey Road* album from 1969 is structured almost exactly the same way as the second side of *Shine On Brightly*, starting with a quiet song independent of the following long sequence, which consists of seemingly unrelated tracks shaped into a whole and rounded off by a flamboyant finale with a guitar solo in the middle.

But Procol Harum were influential on a broader level as well. It has been suggested that the idea of a partnership like the one Brooker-Reid had established could have been an inspiration for Elton John's embarking on a similar relationship with lyric writer Bernie Taupin.

Besides that, there is the whole so-called "progressive" scene, which might never have happened in quite the same way without the efforts of Procol Harum. Out of this particular musical style branched hard rock - which soon developed into heavy rock - and though Procol Harum never had the macho image necessary to be even remotely "heavy" they certainly seem to have had an influence on bands such as Deep Purple and Atomic Rooster.

On the whole, however, British groups who more directly tried to emulate the band's sound were few and far between, apart from what seems like the inevitable attempts to copy "A Whiter Shade Of Pale" (such as "Reflections By Charles Brown", a single released in 1967 on Columbia by a group called Rupert's People). Furthermore, a band called The Ice recorded two remarkably fine singles for Decca in 1967 and 1968, "Anniversary (Of Love)" and "Ice Man", which both came close to Procol Harum in musical style.

In mainland Europe the group's influence was stronger, partly because of their touring there from early on, partly because of their pronounced Gothic feel. In Denmark a group named Ache recorded and released "Shadow Of A Gipsy", an excellent Harum-esque single which won them a silver disc in France. It took Holland's Focus a few years to get it right, but when it happened they did even better with a style that was very much their own but nevertheless had a strong Procol Harum feel to it.

Equally impressive were Wigwam, formed in Helsinki in 1968 and soon joined by expatriate Englishman Jim Pembroke. The group carried on until 1977 and released some very fine records, including three albums for Virgin records. Wigwam's prolific output can be recommended to any follower of Procol Harum.

Like their heroes, Wigwam also featured a two-keyboard line-up (facilitating "live" renditions of songs like "Quite Rightly So" and "A Salty Dog"). This was one area where nearly everyone else fell short. Not only the expense but also the impracticality of incorporating both an organ and a piano made it almost certain that Procol Harum would remain untouched by most competition.

A surprising exception from this rule came with the formation of Freedom in the autumn of 1967. Named after the Charlie Mingus composition which had also been The Paramounts' last recording at Abbey Road, this group featured ex-Procol Harum members Bobby Harrison and Ray Royer. Not just the personnel connections but also a strong similarity in style makes the early history of Freedom relevant here.

I have said earlier that Bobby Harrison and Ray Royer weren't the musical no-hopers they have sometimes been made out to be. The initial idea that Procol Harum could be more-or-less a British answer to what Bob Dylan was doing in the mid-sixties made them both pretty well-suited to the job. However, it is my conclusion from listening to Procol Harum's early attempts to record an album that there was a collision of styles. It turned out that the music was in many ways completely different from Dylan's, and that Bob Dylan's laissez-faire approach was badly suited to the tight structures of Brooker-Reid's compositions, which instead called for extremely disciplined, precise players (just listen to the shambolic version of "Salad Days" by the early line-up featured as a bonus-track on Westside's CD version of the group's first album).

So one of the ideas behind Freedom was for Harrison and Royer to be able to play in a looser style. Through an advert in *Melody Maker* they hired 20 year-old bass player Steve Shirley, who had a good singing voice somewhere between Stevie Winwood and Gary Brooker. Furthermore, keyboard player Tony Marsh joined, an old friend of Royer's who had previously worked with Screaming Lord Sutch and with The Tornados.

Ray Royer: "We had never even played a gig when, in the autumn of 1967, our manager Jonathan Weston was approached by Italian film director Dino de Laurentiis. He was looking for a group to write and perform the soundtrack for a projected film of his which at that point was titled 'Attraction'. The choice was between either us or Steppenwolf. We got the job but we had to change our keyboard player in the process. Our management then came back with Mike Lease, who was an absolute genius."

To my mind the resulting album, titled *Black On White*, is yet another must for any serious Procol Harum follower. Steve Shirley sounds uncannily like Gary Brooker in places, and it is obvious that Mike Lease comes from a background similar to that of Matthew Fisher. One track on the LP is even titled "The Truth Is Plain To See"! But there are other influences which separate Freedom from Procol Harum: a cooking beat, a funky feel for which Bobby Harrison must mainly be held responsible. Finally, Ray Royer's delicate, psychedelic guitar work is miles away from the strict blues playing of Robin Trower.

Sadly, this version of Freedom didn't last long. Mike Lease returned to his native Wales and took up teaching music. Sometime in 1968 Royer and Shirley also left, after which Bobby Harrison regrouped Freedom with guitarist Roger Saunders and bass player Walter Monagham. With this line-up the band went for a harder and more blues/rock orientated style that was a far spell from Procol Harum. However, Harrison continued to move on the fringes of the group. In 1973 he was featured as backing vocalist on Matthew Fisher's first solo album, "Journey's End", and likewise Fisher appeared on Harrison's own solo LP, "Funkist". Around the same time the Procol Harum ex-drummer also formed Snafu, which included keyboard player Pete Solley, who later went on to join Procol Harum in 1976.

It's a dog's life

Nobody understood anyone else in the band. That was the very strange thing.

David Knights

Shine On Brightly was released in the US in September 1968 and went to number 24 in the charts there. Despite some fine reviews in the UK, the album didn't even enter its homeland's charts, a clear confirmation that Procol Harum's main territory was to be found "across the pond". The fact that the UK edition wasn't released until December didn't help things either.

A single "Quite Rightly So" was backed by a non-LP track "In The Wee Small Hours Of Sixpence", presumably a left-over from the earliest days of the Brooker-Reid partnership. This was yet another lyric with a structure almost exactly the same as "A Whiter Shade Of Pale". Unsurprisingly, it features some great singing and organ playing, but the piano solo in the break seems to disappear somewhat in the mix, turning what should have been a climax into a strange non-event.

Incidentally, the Scandinavian version of the record featured a different lyric on the A-side, and on the B-side an alternative mix of "Rambling On". Another unusual single came out in Italy and featured Gary Brooker singing "Shine On Brightly" in Italian (since he doesn't speak the language he had to learn the lines one by one phonetically as the recording went along). Disappointingly the B-side, "Fortuna", turns out to be our old friend "Repent Walpurgis" in disguise. On all these four sides the instrumental backing is the same as on the standard UK versions.

When Procol Harum returned to England from American in early 1969 with the intention of recording their third album, they brought with them two 10" acetates containing three songs produced by one of their own members. These tracks were "Wreck Of The Hesperus" in an early mix without orchestral overdubs, "Long Gone Geek" without acoustic guitar overdubs, and a long instrumental track somewhat in the style of "Repent Walpurgis" which had been given the working title "Stoke Poges". These tracks had all been recorded at Wally Heider's Studio 3 in Los Angeles on 8-track equipment. The producer was Matthew Fisher:

"From way back when I was at music school my intention had been to become a producer, and I thought there were three ways I could do this. One was just to go to music school, come out with my qualifications and apply directly to a record company. In fact, that probably wouldn't have worked very well at all. It sort of worked in the days of George Martin – that's how he got his job – but times had changed a hell of a lot since then. The other two ways were, I thought, through being an engineer or something, then working up that way, or through being in some band that may have had a couple of successful records or whatever, and get in that way. I made a few efforts of seeing if there were any jobs going for trainee engineers, because at that time I felt that I had the right sort of qualifications for it, and met with no luck at all. So I thought, 'Oh, I'll just go back to playing in bands then.' Obviously, the third way turned out to be the possible one."

The three tracks recorded in Los Angeles were to serve as a test that Fisher could actually handle the job. It was indeed unusual for bands at the time to have one of their own members producing their records. Nevertheless, it was decided that Matthew Fisher had done a good job and that he should go ahead.

The band entered Abbey Road Studios and to their surprise found that other groups recording there at the time – mainly The Beatles and The Shadows – had left an abundance of unusual instruments behind. This was to have a huge influence on Procol Harum's own record.

"You could get all the odd instruments out like xylophones, which they didn't have at Olympic," Brooker told Chris Welch in 1997. "It gave us a bit more scope and there is a very colourful sound on this record."

As a forerunner for the album a single featuring the title track, "A Salty Dog", was released in June 1969. Many followers of the group still consider it their "finest hour".

Gary Brooker remembers that, "It was our first attempt to work with an orchestra. I had no training really when it came to writing scores. I just taught myself and then a friend of mine, who played the violin, helped me a bit. He would show me what was actually possible to play on that instrument. When the recording came along I even conducted the orchestra, though I really hadn't a clue how to do it. I just waved my hands in the air. The orchestra were such resourceful people, all leaders of orchestras and that sort of thing. Very skilful."

The lyric starts with a ship and its crew running "afloat", the reversed term suggesting that not hitting land but going to sea is a catastrophe. The voyage itself is only superficially described, but at least we are told that it goes to places where no man has been before, and that it is a winding journey. Furthermore, it is divulged that the trip will inevitably end with the whole crew dying.

As mentioned earlier Reid uses the sea as a metaphor for life itself, which is always portrayed as a bewildered and threatened situation. The description here of what happens afterwards is very sparse. Reid is no prophet.

Perhaps the most important bit of information about the journey itself is given in one of the last lines of the song, where we are told that being a "salty dog" is the essence of the narrator's life story, his "log". It is probably not irrelevant that "salty dog" is an old term for a lusty sailor. The phrase occurs in folk songs on both sides of the Atlantic, the narrator typically pleading with his female friend that if she won't marry him, at least she can allow him to be her "salty dog" for a night or two.

I hesitate to take this interpretation much further because line-by-line analysis of Keith Reid's songs always puts the reader on shaky ground. One reason for this could be that as a lyric writer Reid has many more agendas to consider than just communicating views and feelings; he has to incorporate rhymes, while also paying attention to both rhythm and sound. Furthermore, Keith Reid has always been extremely reluctant to reveal anything about his personal life and what is on his mind. Consequently, to understand his lyrics it is crucial to concentrate on the overall, repetitive themes, which on this album are not terribly different from his previous work, apart from what seems to be a drift towards an increasingly desperate mood.

It is this mood, the life/death topic, which Gary Brooker picks up on musically by giving the title track an almost other-worldly feel. However, the earthy sailor theme is ignored, which is perhaps what frustrated Keith Reid at the time:

"Lots of times, initially I didn't like the music because I had a certain thing in mind and it came out a different way and it would take me a while to see that it was really good. Like 'Salty Dog', I remember initially I thought it should have a different kind of music. Gary wrote it in Switzerland, I think. He played it for me and I can remember I didn't think, 'Wow, that's fantastic.' But then after a while, when I got rid of my preconceptions about it, I thought it was great. I thought it was one of the best songs that we ever wrote."

Apart from the string arrangement, the instrumental backing is very much a collaboration between piano, drums and bass. BJ Wilson's playing is so astonishingly creative it is easy to understand why so many attempts were made to lure him away throughout Procol Harum's career (around this time it was Jimmy Page who tried to tempt Wilson into becoming a member of the New Yardbirds, who soon afterwards changed their name to Led Zeppelin). Matthew Fisher isn't on the recording at all, and Robin Trower is relegated to playing a faintly-heard acoustic guitar.

The "A Salty Dog" single became a minor hit in several countries, even in Britain. Followers of the group often complain that it deserved to be a much bigger seller, but perhaps it is more remarkable that a song which has practically nothing in common with commercial pop records managed to make its way into the charts at all.

The B-side is an outright rocker, "Long Gone Geek", with Reid in his weirdest mood, almost like a sinister Lewis Carroll. Matthew Fisher remembers that, "About a year or so earlier on we had been recording in a studio next to The Small Faces. It was so nice to go in there and be with them, because everyone was having such a good time, whereas with us it was always very gloomy. I thought, 'Hell, let's write a song like the Small Faces'. So we wrote and recorded 'Long Gone Geek'."

The song started off as a jam session, with Keith Reid writing the words for it later. After the group's return to England, Matthew Fisher added an acoustic guitar which to my mind takes some of the edge off the overall feel. However, that is only a minor complaint; the song really ought to have been an A-side.

The idea of writing the music first and then adding the lyrics was relatively new to the band and indicates that something was starting to change within Procol Harum.

"People wanted to do more," Keith Reid told me. "Robin wanted to write, Matthew wanted to write, and it ended up being a real group record. Everybody was just doing a lot more... There were five people all with something really strong to say individually, and that was why people left to do other things."

The front sleeve for *A Salty Dog* is based on a well-known logo used by the tobacco company Players for their "Navy Cut". It is the second out of three Procol Harum album covers designed by Keith Reid's girlfriend Dickinson, who by now he had married.

The main feature is a torso of a sailor inside a lifebelt. While the original sailor on the Players logo was rather idealised, Dickinson seems to have replaced him with a painting of her husband wearing a wild, unkempt beard and a not particularly trustworthy expression on his face. Perhaps the likeness isn't entirely obvious, but at least the characteristic profile and the shape of the lips are easily recognisable. Keith Reid apparently himself suggested the overall idea of the design for the album.

The back of the sleeve states the instrumentation played by each member of the group, but it doesn't relate this information to the individual songs. Therefore, the LP is worth a track by track examination.

The "A Salty Dog" single was in mono while the album was mixed in stereo only. The instrumentation on the single has already been delved into, but perhaps it is worth mentioning that the wonderfully strange chord beginning the song was inspired by the sound of a locomotive whistle Brooker had heard during a holiday in Switzerland where he was writing the music.

"The Milk Of Human Kindness" is a typical Keith Reid love-gone-wrong story with a feeling of bitterness, anger and self-pity. The narrator admits to having committed some kind of a mistake (we can only guess what) but complains that his partner is taking it out on him much too harshly. She is compared with a snake while he is but a wasp. Musically, the line-up is business as usual.

However, the following track "Too Much Between Us" is instrumentally quite a different affair (unlike the lyric, where the subject could easily be the very same "affair" as referred to on the previous track). Here we have Brooker on celeste and three string guitar (sic). The whole band sing along during the chorus. BJ Wilson's drumming is absent, Fisher plays Hammond, and Robin Trower is back on acoustic guitar. He is also the co-writer of the song together with Gary Brooker.

Keith Reid told Chris Welch that "Too Much Between Us" is "a love song about somebody who was in New York while I was in London. It's written like a letter."

Matthew Fisher swaps his Hammond for an electric rhythm guitar on "The Devil Came From Kansas", according to Keith Reid a lyric inspired by a Randy Newman song called "The Beehive State" (I personally fail to see much of a connection).

It has been suggested that Reid around this time was embarking on some kind of flirtation with witchcraft (see Sam Cameron's essay at the *Beyond The Pale* Website, *Nothing Called Not Name Or Number*), something that wasn't unusual for people involved in rock 'n' roll circles during the late sixties and early seventies. Here we certainly have a clear reference to the Devil along with some frightening surreal imagery. The narrator announces that while he has previously been lost he is now able to "look"; he has even found a turning at the notorious signpost (which wasn't of much use to him in "Homburg" and "Shine On Brightly"), a road which takes him to a pool inside a forest where he shall apparently drown.

While this is not enough for me to be convinced by the witchcraft theory, I nevertheless see the eerie aspects. There is a dreamy, monochrome, grainy atmosphere to this song. Musically, the chorus repeatedly transposes into subdominants, an unusual feature which Buddy Holly also utilised on his famous song "Everyday"; but while Holly is wholesome, this is a report from a disintegrating universe.

The final track on side one is "Boredom", a musical collaboration between Brooker and Fisher, and a song about mildly bewildered resignation. It features Fisher taking over on lead vocal. He furthermore plays acoustic guitar, recorder and marimba. Robin Trower beats a sleigh tambourine, Brooker plays recorder and sings backing vocals, while BJ Wilson goes all exotic on conga drums and tabla.

Turning the record over we are treated to some old fashioned country blues and a lyric with strong religious connotations, a pronounced feeling of guilt, and a fear of eternal damnation. The overall spirit is of coldness, regret and lack of mercy – garnished with a pinch of black humour. The music is by Robin Trower; Gary Brooker sings and plays harp harmonica, while the electric guitar of "Throbbin' Robin" is the only other featured instrument. The rest of the group, along with friends and roadies, keep themselves busy stamping the floor and hitting cardboard boxes.

"The Wreck Of The Hesperus" is another song where the music was written before the lyric. It is a Matthew Fisher composition which he sings himself. The intricate piano part had to be split between him and Gary Brooker (Fisher played the right hand, Brooker the left). Matthew Fisher also wrote the very ambitious and highly-accomplished score, and once again the orchestra was conducted by Gary Brooker.

He remains on the podium for the next treat, "All This And More", a grand composition augmented by horns and some amazing guitar work. "Rob didn't seem to know what the chords were half of the time," BJ Wilson once declared. "But he would just play stuff that fitted so well."

Robin Trower takes over the lead vocal duties on "Crucifiction Lane", which he wrote the music for, perhaps the strongest comment Keith Reid has ever made on feeling insignificant and fearful.

Both Trower and Matthew Fisher are reasonable vocalists, and Fisher's voice in particular has interesting timbres, but most people would have problems with appearing as singers alongside Gary Brooker. Nevertheless, it makes for some nice variation here and both Trower and Fisher go for a more vibrant and emotional delivery, perhaps to compensate for not being as technically talented as Gary Brooker.

Like the first two LPs this one ends with a Matthew Fisher composition. "Pilgrim's Progress" has all his trademarks including the dense, dominant Hammond sound and a melodic, vulnerable vocal delivery.

Brooker plays the piano and is furthermore in there somewhere on woods. Lots of hand claps from the rest of the band, roadies and friends, even some single notes hammered out on a tubular bell.

As stated earlier by Gary Brooker *A Salty Dog* is an extremely varied LP. In fact, some people find too much variation on it and have criticised it for sounding almost like a compilation album of different artists.

My opinion is the exact opposite. To me the fact that this album sounds so integrated, despite being based on the work of three different songwriters and singers, suggests two points. First, that the producer managed to tie everything together pretty well. Second, that underneath a surface of disputes and differences, personal as well as musical, there existed in Procol Harum a deeper, artistic consensus.

1969 didn't just mark the year when Procol Harum recorded perhaps their finest album. It was also the year when they appeared for the first time "live" on stage with a symphony orchestra.

This concert took place in connection with the Shakespeare Festival in Stratford, Ontario, Canada where the group performed the song cycle "In Held 'Twas In I". I shall return to this remarkable event later on when dealing with Harum's many concerts in this kind of setting, particularly the 1971 "live" recording with the Edmonton Symphony Orchestra, which was released and became the band's best-ever selling album.

Unfortunately, even artistic successes such as the *A Salty Dog* LP and the Stratford concert weren't enough to carry the classic line-up of the group into the 1970s.

The disagreement between Gary Brooker and Matthew Fisher over the royalties for "A Whiter Shade Of Pale" has already been mentioned. According to Fisher, Keith Reid refused to take sides on this issue at the time. But there also seems to have been a potential rivalry between Fisher and Reid.

Matthew Fisher has stated that one of his reasons for leaving Procol Harum was that all songs written for the group had to have lyrics by Keith Reid:

"We were all very pleased with Keith's lyrics, they were obviously very good and unusual and interesting. But when it's been going on for years and years and the guy comes up with the next batch and it's all about the same old coffins and rotting corpses and what have you all over again, it tends to put you off a bit."

Both Matthew Fisher and Robin Trower seemed to be gradually taking over some of Brooker's responsibilities in Procol Harum. I doesn't seem to have bothered Gary Brooker; on the contrary, he encouraged it. But it also appears that Fisher felt the urge to step into Keith Reid's domain and start writing some lyrics of his own. In Procol Harum such a thing was out of the question, and Matthew Fisher's frustration grew.

Gary Brooker: "I remember Matthew moaning and wanting to leave in about the fourth week [after forming the band], and he went on moaning and wanting to leave until eventually we only had to agree that it would be best."

"He was always gonna leave right from when I joined," said Robin Trower. "That was the thing, he didn't wanna be in Procol Harum... But he was good, so good on the organ. Brilliant, you know. He had a sound, he had a touch. He's just a great musician."

I once asked Matthew Fisher's then-wife Linda if she could recall the exact occasion when her husband finally made up his mind to leave Procol Harum.

"I do, I remember it well," she said. "We were standing in a parking lot in Los Angeles on a very hot day, and Matthew told Dave that he'd finally made up his mind. We then went for a walk together all three of us and I recall that Dave kept saying, 'If Matthew's leaving I'm leaving too.'"

Dave Knights told me that he had a feeling at this point that if he didn't go voluntarily he would be told to leave, a view which seems to be true. "I think it's a shame that when the original line-up ended it couldn't have gone on. But it couldn't have gone on without some major change. I think that if for example it had gone into a lot more feel, a lot more driving force, with rougher edges, not so arranged – that could have been quite an exciting situation."

It may have surprised some fans that Robin Trower didn't leave the group at the same time, since he was obviously gaining more confidence in his own playing and composing abilities. In the late sixties Britain went through the so-called Blues Boom, and it is strange to think that during those years one of the nation's best blues guitarists found himself stuck between two keyboards and a set of baroque chord sequences.

"As a guitarist Rob must have felt terribly frustrated," said David Knights. "A guitarist needs to open up, and he couldn't because it was very much of a framework... Until '67-'68 I suppose he was falling in line with what was needed. By 1969 I detected that he was getting a little bit frustrated. I suppose that he got more confidence because he started to write, and perhaps he became a little more demanding."

But Robin Trower stayed on, and Brooker and Reid decided to continue, taking the group into a whole new era. Despite his constant threats to leave, Matthew Fisher had stayed in the band long enough to build himself a platform from which he could launch his own career as a producer and a solo artist. But in the meantime the rest of the group had also developed musically to a point where they were able to carry on without him. Ironically, the production on *A Salty Dog*, with its surprising lack of organ, was a sign that perhaps Procol Harum actually had a future ahead of them even without their second-to-none Hammond wizard.

Part Four

Holding On, 1969-1972

Rob the tower

Q: How many bass players does it take to change a light bulb?
A: You don't need any bass players to change a light bulb. The organ player can do it with his left hand.

With the departure of Fisher and Knights the remaining members of Procol Harum found themselves standing at a crossroads.

"The thing is, you couldn't replace Matthew," concluded Robin Trower, who was instrumental in the band's decision to become a four-piece. "So you more-or-less had to come up with a different way of doing it. We decided that the best thing would be not to have so much organ in the sound."

Gary Brooker: "It may have been an underhand method of Rob Trower's, perhaps to get a little more limelight."

As a replacement for both Fisher and Knights, Chris Copping was suggested. If he accepted it would mean that the group became an all ex-Paramounts line-up (though it must be emphasised that apart from one single occasion BJ Wilson and Chris Copping had never played in The Paramounts together, having been members at different times).

I asked Gary Brooker if there had been a deliberate plan to reform the old group. "It was certainly not intended as that," he said. "Chris was a known good keyboard player and also a bass player, and the intention was that he did both things. I think it was a little bit wishful thinking that it was possible."

Since leaving The Paramounts some six years earlier Chris Copping had been busy building an academic career. From 1963 until 1966 he was a student at Leicester University, where he took an Honours Degree in Chemistry. Between 1966 and 1969 he was working for the British Government and doing a Ph.D.

In the meantime Copping's first marriage had broken up and he had also started to play music again, first as an organist in a London pub and later in a band playing traditional German music in a club. It wasn't exactly progressive rock, but it got him active on the playing front again. By now he felt tempted to get back into music despite having only one year left to go before earning his Ph.D.

Then in the summer of 1969, when he was working in a laboratory in Walton Abbey on the outskirts of North London, Copping received a phone call that would change his life completely. The caller was his old pal Robin Trower, offering him a position as a member of Procol Harum. Copping immediately agreed to join.

No audition needed to be held. Instead, the first thing the band did was to secure access to a hall for rehearsals and get hold of a bass and an amplifier for their new man.

To begin with they were just a trio; Trower, Wilson and Chris Copping plunking away until Copping got blisters on his fingers. He hadn't played electric bass for quite a while!

Soon after it all got a bit more serious. The group rented a cottage in Sussex for rehearsals, and during those snowy winter days of late 1969 a documentary was filmed for Australian television.

Four new songs were presented in the documentary – "The Dead Man's Dream", "Whisky Train", "Nothing That I Didn't Know" and "Piggy Pig Pig". These songs all ended up on the *Home* album, but the versions used in the film came from some earlier attempts to record the LP. At this point Matthew Fisher, though no longer a group member, still worked as Procol Harum's producer.

Around the same time the band was also asked to play as a backing group on a single by legendary Southend rock 'n' roller Mickey Jupp, whose manager at this point was none other than ex-Procol Harum bassist Dave Knights.

It has often been assumed that Chris Copping played the bass on these recordings. However, Matthew Fisher informed me that this was not the case.

"I played bass on both tracks," he said. "They were using BJ on drums and the feeling at the time was that if they had BJ *and* Chris it would just be too much Procol Harum."

The resulting single, "Georgia George Part 1", released under the name of Legend (see discography), would be the last recording featuring Matthew Fisher and Procol Harum until the 1991 reunion.

While on the subject of session work it is worth mentioning that this was far from the only case where Procol Harum members acted as backing players for other artists. Already in 1967 BJ Wilson had played on Joe Cocker's famous version of the Lennon-McCartney composition "With A Little Help From My Friends" – furthermore, both Wilson and Matthew Fisher played on another Joe Cocker track, a version of Bob Dylan's "Just Like A Woman" (both tracks are featured on the album *With A Little Help From My Friends*, Regal Zonophone SLRZ 1006, 1969).

Fisher also played piano on three recordings by The Move: "Fire Brigade" (Regal Zonophone RZ 3005, 1968), "Hey Grandma" (a track on the LP *The Move*, (S)LRZ 1002, 1968), and "Brontosaurus" (RZ 3026, 1970).

Gary Brooker was a session pianist on George Harrison's triple album, *All Things Must Pass* (Apple STCH 639, 1971).

"I played on two tracks, 'Wah Wah' and 'My Sweet Lord'," he remembered. "It was a huge band, Phil Spector producing. I loved it. It was a good session. Eric Clapton, myself, Bobby Whitlock, Ringo on the drums, Klaus Voormann on bass, Badfinger playing the acoustic guitars, and about four madmen playing percussion – quite a big outfit. George on guitar!"

Going back to the situation in late 1969, things weren't going well between Procol Harum and their producer. "I got half way through the album and then relations got a bit strained between me and the band," Matthew Fisher told me.

Gary Brooker remembers that, "We weren't getting on with Matthew, I don't think. The group didn't like what he was doing. Yeah, that didn't work out that time with Matthew."

Hence Matthew Fisher and the group agreed to part ways and the band started shopping around for a new producer.

"We wanted Glyn Johns to produce us and he didn't wanna know!" said Keith Reid. "I think maybe we even tried to get George Martin...

I can remember we tried to get a lot of different people but all the people we wanted didn't wanna do it, and we were recommended we should try out this guy Chris Thomas. I think we were persuaded to give him a try, and he was great... we were very, very happy when we started to work with him."

A student of The Beatles' famous producer, George Martin, Chris Thomas had been a session player on the 1968 double LP *The Beatles*, better known as *The White Album* (he contributed the harpsichord on George Harrison's "Piggies"). Later on in the seventies Thomas would go on to win himself much acclaim as a producer for Elton John and many others – he was even partly responsible for launching the punk phenomenon on record in 1976 when the Sex Pistols recorded their first album using him as their producer. Back in 1969/70, however, Chris Thomas was still largely unknown within the music business and his work for Procol Harum would to a certain extent become a test piece for his further career.

Before starting to record a new version of *Home* the group laid down another session which in time would become a legend among their followers. It featured a large number of songs from The Paramounts' old repertoire.

"It was in about January 1970," Gary Brooker said. "We went into the EMI studios one night and we recorded about 40 songs. What happened then was that Chris Thomas mixed I think about 20 of them and the tape was around for a while. That was me, BJ, Copping and Trower."

The cream of the January 1970 rock 'n' roll session finally became officially available in 1998 via Gary Brooker's own label Gazza Records and the fan-club *Shine On* (a smaller selection of the tracks is featured on EMI's *The Paramounts At Abbey Road*). The compact disc – titled *Ain't Nothing To Get Excited About* and released under the name of Liquorice John Death – once again supports the view that underneath the experimenting attitudes and "progressiveness" Procol Harum always remained a down-to-earth rhythm 'n' blues band.

Liquorice John Death was a nickname for The Paramounts invented by one of their long-standing fans, Dave Mundy. For the sake of completeness it can be revealed that Mundy also had nicknames for the individual members of the group – Gary Brooker was *Liquorice John Death*, Robin Trower was *Humdrum Pete*, Chris Copping was *Chris*

"The Man" C, and BJ Wilson *Shaky Jake*. Finally, the visiting sax player on the session, Jack Lancaster, was *Jack The Lad*.

Dave Mundy furthermore wrote the words for "Well I...", the only non-Reid lyric set to music and performed by Procol Harum at this point (the song was played on their 1970 tour and on BBC sessions). He also designed a sleeve for the album at the time, indicating that there were at least at some level plans of a release. Sadly, Dave Mundy committed suicide in 1972, prompting Keith Reid to write the song "For Liquorice John" which appeared the following year on the *Grand Hotel* album.

While the compact disc features thirteen songs from the session, it remains somewhat uncertain what else was recorded on that day. Brooker's recollection of putting down 40 tracks is probably exaggerated. I have on other occasions heard him mention 24, "of which half got mixed". Furthermore, Chris Thomas ran a rough mix straight on to two tracks as the recordings were going on. Some of these tapes still exist and feature at least four (very poorly mixed) songs which are not on the CD – "No Money Down", "I Just Wanna Make Love To You", "Willie & The Hand Jive" and "Too Much Monkey Business".

The group now finally set about re-recording their follow-up album to *A Salty Dog*. Lyrically, it would strike the critics as extremely "death-orientated".

"I wasn't aware of it," said Keith Reid. "It was only when people starting going on about it and I looked at the lyrics and saw – but I didn't realise that at all. It was pointed out to me and I looked – but that was totally subconscious. Totally."

In the Chris Welch interview, Reid admits to feeling a lack of inspiration when writing for the new album. He also agrees that *Home* is an exceedingly depressed record:

"It was quite doomy. Very much so. When I listen to it now it seems incredibly dark. At the time I probably wasn't aware of it, but in retrospect I must have been going through a deeply depressed state. The band was in a lot of turmoil."

One thing that is striking about the album is that, although it immediately comes across as nowhere near as musically varied as its predecessor, it nevertheless seems much more inconsistent. The problem is that rather than being multi-faceted this LP consists of two distinctively different kinds of songs pulling in different directions.

There is one group of tracks here which are like the old Procol Harum and in fact could easily have appeared on *Shine On Brightly*, such as "The Dead Man's Dream", "Nothing That I Didn't Know" (featuring an accordion, played by Brooker), "Barnyard Story" (which has Chris Copping playing an upright acoustic bass) and "Whaling Stories". These songs have a strong majestic feel, simple bass playing, and a dominant organ (in the case of "Barnyard Stories" actually a harmonium).

Then there is another category of tracks – like "Whisky Train", "Still There'll Be More" and "Your Own Choice" (featuring Larry Adler on harp harmonica) – which have no organ at all. These songs are more upbeat, almost funky with a lot of guitar, a cooking rhythm, and some pretty energetic bass playing (Chris Copping was into soul bands like Sly and the Family Stone). Only "About To Die" and "Piggy Pig Pig" manage to embrace both styles at the same time.

It goes without saying that with an LP of this nature the track listing is crucial. Procol Harum, being an album-oriented band, were always aware of the importance of track sequences and spent a lot of time getting them right. However, in this particular case I don't think they succeeded very well.

The album starts with "Whisky Train", which is like nothing else on the LP and thus sets a completely irrelevant mood. It features some fantastic soloing from Robin Trower, who also wrote the music, but it is hardly the best song the group ever recorded (in fact, I find it marred by endless repetitions of a not particularly inventive guitar riff). Even worse, it is followed by "The Dead Man's Dream", which sounds so different that only the vocal confirms that this is the same group.

Throughout the LP the band continue to set and break moods in a similarly reckless manner, which could quite easily have been avoided by a better track listing. On the German edition of the album this was partly rectified by letting "The Dead Man's Dream" swap places with "Your Own Choice". However, that wasn't quite enough to create a wholly consistent album.

Luckily the problem is partly solved with the advent of the compact disc, as listeners now can programme their own running order. In the case of *Home* I would suggest the following track listing (to compare with the old vinyl LP I have maintained the structure of having two different sides on a record):

Side 1. Still There'll Be More, About To Die, The Dead Man's Dream, Piggy Pig Pig, Whisky Train.

Side 2. Your Own Choice, Nothing That I Didn't Know, Barnyard Story, Whaling Stories.

One of the many advantages of this alternative running order is that it rounds off the album with one of the group's best-ever songs, "Whaling Stories". With each of its verses set to a different piece of music this triumphant composition is the closest Procol Harum ever got to being a progressive rock band in the vein of groups such as Genesis or Yes. Thanks to Gary Brooker's musical intuition he left it at that and never tried to take the concept any further (unless you insist on including 1977's "The Worm And The Tree", which was to signal the demise of the group). Good ideas only remain good as long as you don't overdo them...

Not just the track-listing but other things went wrong on *Home* as well, some of which could have been just as easily avoided. For instance, if the title bears any relevance to the music on the album it is too convoluted to recognise (at least for me), and the sleeve in all its stark, laboured naivety seems more concerned with the designer, Dickinson again, making her own private statements about the personality of each group member than with reflecting the music in any way.

On a more positive note, *Home* signals an important development in Reid's work. Apart from "Barnyard Story", which once again refers to some kind of quasi-religious experience, the well-known existentialist/atheist themes are replaced by a kind of intelligent man's horror stories where parallels to Edgar Allen Poe seem more obvious than those to Franz Kafka or Bob Dylan.

In 1997 Keith Reid told Chris Welch about "The Dead Man's Dream": "When I listen to it now, I wish we had never recorded it, as it seems so depressing. It's supposed to be some sort of Gothic fairy tale I think... I remember when we did the John Peel Show on BBC Radio we were going to play 'The Dead Man's Dream' and he objected! The producer came up to us and said that John didn't want the song played on his show. He probably doesn't remember it now...

there was a blazing row in the studio about censorship, but he thought it was morbid and he was probably right."

Musically the album leans more on Robin Trower than ever before. Since *A Salty Dog* he had obviously been undergoing a tremendous development on the technical front, while still maintaining his "feel".

Home also marks the point were Trower starts working with effects, particularly on "Your Own Choice" and "About To Die". Coincidentally, Paul McCartney was recording "Maybe I'm Amazed" in the same studio (Abbey Road) at the time, and he had experimented with plugging a guitar into a Lesley organ speaker. "He'd just about clapped the Lesley out," recalled Chris Copping, "giving it a resultant sound which was perfect for what we wanted."

While Chris Copping's double role in the band caused no problems in the studio – it was just a case of using overdubbing technique – it was quite a different matter when the band was playing "live". Becoming a four-piece led to a lot of moving around on stage. Piano and drums were fixed features, but everything else was constantly changing.

If the band wanted the full sound of guitar, organ and bass, Chris Copping would use his left hand to play a keyboard bass resting on top of the Hammond. As this meant he could play only the top manual of the Hammond the sound was not as powerful as when Matthew Fisher had been in the group, but it was nevertheless the best possible solution for certain numbers such as "Shine On Brightly" and "Whaling Stories".

Other songs, like "A Salty Dog" and "Homburg", didn't feature much guitar in the first place and therefore Robin Trower would switch over and play the bass guitar. In such instances Copping would just play his Hammond, so the group got a bigger sound since he now had both his hands available for the organ manuals.

If the band were doing something that was more rocking, like "Whisky Train" and other songs where the organ could be left out and instead the feel of a proper bass guitar was called for, Copping would step off the organ and just play the bass.

Understandably, Chris Copping wasn't comfortable with the situation. In particular the keyboard bass was awful – the other members called it "the fart machine".

Consequently, the band's "live" sound wasn't particularly impressive around this time. They played a pretty harsh sounding set at the Isle of Wight Festival, from which "A Salty Dog" was later released (see discography). Likewise a much-bootlegged "live" FM radio broadcast from Philadelphia, USA in 1971 sounds a bit of a mess, its most uplifting moment being a full band rendition of "Juicy John Pink".

To confuse things even more there was also a version of the line-up where Keith Reid would join in as a player.

"I played organ on stage a couple of times," he admitted. "I played organ on 'About To Die' and 'Piggy Pig Pig'. I can remember we played at the Lyceum with The Rolling Stones and we did 'Piggy Pig Pig'. I played on stage on that."

Reid furthermore played on the same tracks in the studio when *Home* was recorded, although he wasn't credited on the album insert. But Keith Reid never felt comfortable with being Procol Harum's organ player, and neither did Robin Trower with playing bass.

"It was all just helping out, really," Trower told me. "I wasn't mad about that, but you just do whatever it takes to make the thing work. In those days things weren't so tight. You didn't have to do the big show thing so much."

It was nevertheless during these years that the band started to become more of a "live" act.

Keith Reid: "We toured all the time in America. Earlier on people liked us a lot in Detroit, and we got a really strong following there and we always seemed to be playing in Detroit, like every three months. But really we were working in America 'cause it was the only place we could work in. And we just did lots of tours there, we were just touring there all the time."

The recording of *Broken Barricades* began at George Martin's AIR Studios in Oxford Street, London during February 1971. It would be Robin Trower's last record with the group before breaking off to start his own band.

With just a week between ending an American tour and going in to record, a lot of the new material had to be written as the group went along.

"Making the *Home* album was all right of course," Gary Brooker stated, "because you can have all the instruments on it in the studio.

But once we got out on the road, after about a year it was not quite satisfying with this keyboard bass. And so by the time we got around to doing *Broken Barricades* we had really become more of a four-piece and I think you'd have a lot of trouble picking out any organ on *Broken Barricades*. The only significant development of Procol Harum on that album was obviously that Trower clicked in his mind and found that now was the time when he was ready to go and do his own thing. It particularly seemed to come about from 'Song For A Dreamer'."

Robin Trower recalls, "'Song For A Dreamer' was just a talking thing. That was an atmosphere, and that did come off. I really like that track. In fact, it was that track that led me down to the path that I eventually followed."

What Robin Trower partly refers to here is a profound inspiration from Jimi Hendrix which over the years would fuel his work as the leader of his own trio.

"I only had one of his albums when he died. I wasn't a follower of his. I liked his first album and that was it, and I lost contact with him as far as an artist goes after that because I was more interested in blues and black music; that's always been my main diet of music. Just after he died we went to America and I was sitting in a hotel bedroom fooling with a funny tuning on the guitar and I came up with this idea that I thought could be a song. Just as I'd formulated it Keith walked in and said, 'I got this lyric. It's a tribute to Hendrix.' It was 'Song For A Dreamer'. I said, 'Let's have a look at it,' and it fitted perfectly to this music. So it was just one of those things that was meant to be. The die was cast."

Before doing any more work on the song Trower sat down and listened carefully to all Hendrix's records.

"I really studied it a lot to make it sound as much as possible like the feeling of what he created. So because I did all that it had a terrific impact on me. It wasn't something that I listened to over the years. I heard it all over a period of a few days. I really listened to it all a lot, and it had such an imprint on me that everything I wrote after that started to sound like him. So in one way it was a good thing that I tried to do the tribute to him, but it obviously influenced me more than normal. I think it did have the feeling of some of the stuff he'd done, which is what I set out to do."

Broken Barricades became a critics' pet and got at least two "Best Album Of The Year" accolades – one from John Peel, and another from *The Village Voice*. Though in many ways it is an atypical Procol Harum album it nevertheless remains a favourite with many of the group's followers. Surprisingly Robin Trower, who wrote three of the eight songs on the record and sang lead vocal on two of them, remains humble about his own efforts:

"It was always Gary's things, it was always Gary's group. I just tried to do whatever I could to make it work, put as much as I could into it. I was writing because he wasn't coming up with enough material to do a whole album. If he had I probably wouldn't have bothered presenting my songs."

There is no arguing that *Broken Barricades* was artistically a highly successful LP, and not just because of Robin Trower's contributions. The album opener, "Simple Sister", with its repetitive theme over which layers of single instruments and orchestration (conducted by George Martin) are gradually added, predates Mike Oldfield's *Tubular Bells* by a couple of years and could well have been an inspiration. The post-apocalyptic title track is wonderfully mysterious and, like "Luskus Delph", makes tasteful use of a Moog synthesizer (programmed by Chris Thomas and played by Gary Brooker). The track also has some excellent drumming from BJ Wilson, while the rudely-titled "Playmate Of The Mouth" features a horn section (and Gary Brooker singing with a severe cold!)

Brooker's songwriting on the album is more simplistic than ever before, often built around basic, repetitive chord sequences. The result is impressive and powerful, the track listing this time is perfect, and the sleeve is a satisfyingly precise reflection of the album's overall mood. However, it would have been nice to see *all* the lyrics in print; furthermore, mentioning George Martin's involvement could only have boosted the band's image.

But these are just minor details. My only serious regret is that Gary Brooker's piano playing wasn't brought more to the fore during this period when the group was a quartet. His only two solos, on "About To Die" (on the *Home* album) and "Memorial Drive" (on *Broken Barricades*), sound dull and uninspired. To know what a fine pianist he really is you still had to revert to the old original Paramounts days – a missed potential, indeed.

It took 35 twelve-hour sessions to get *Broken Barricades* right, and work finished at the end of March 1971, once again using Chris Thomas as a producer. After that the group set out on their very first tour of Britain since the days of the Royer/Harrison line-up. As if that were not absurd enough, the tour featured them only as support act for Jethro Tull!

Broken Barricades enjoyed some brief chart success (UK 42, US 32). In Britain it seemed to get somewhat lost in a strange distribution arrangement between Island Records and Chrysalis, to which the group were now signed. While the band saw it as a relief to get away from Regal Zonophone in the UK (*Home* had been their last album for the label), the new situation was not much better to begin with.

Procol Harum had already been with Chrysalis Management for some time and now the company was setting up business as a record label as well. However, the arrangement was not yet consolidated when *Broken Barricades* got released, which explains the trainspotters' mystery of the record ending up on the Chrysalis label while having an Island catalogue number.

The crowd clapped desperately

Most people who turned up for the audition were just a bloody joke. A third of them were idiots. I remember Keith hiding under the piano trying to stop laughing.

Chris Copping (to Bob Lloyd, 1984)

From the outset, Robin Trower's departure from Procol Harum looked to be reasonably amicable. The guitarist even agreed to go on one last tour of the States because it would otherwise cause problems for the band who simply didn't have time enough to find a replacement for him. It was only when Trower suddenly asked BJ Wilson to join his new band, a proposition Wilson agreed to, that panic started to break out.

"We were all fed up with Robin by the time he wanted to leave," Keith Reid remembered. "I know we didn't try and persuade him to stay, whereas with BJ we really persuaded him to stay. If he had left then we would have broken up for sure, because it would have been too difficult."

Eventually BJ Wilson decided to remain in the group. That, however, was only one problem solved. Procol Harum still didn't have a guitarist, and furthermore a solution had to be found to the bass keyboard problem. Gary Brooker recalls that, "I said, 'Guys, let's get back our sound. Let's get the organ going again.'"

A number of different options were debated. First it had to be decided whether Chris Copping should concentrate on his bass or his organ playing. Initially, he opted for the bass.

Consequently Procol Harum went hunting for a guitarist and an organist at the same time, keyboard player Richard Tandy (formerly with The Move, later with ELO) being one of several people who came along to audition.

For some reason this combination didn't work out and as time ticked by and no suitable solution seemed to be within reach things were getting desperate once again. There was a tour schedule to be met in the autumn, and the group still lacked two members.

As they had done many times before, Procol Harum fell back on the tried-and-tested formula of advertising in the music papers.

"There were about eighty applicants for the guitarist job," Brooker told Paul Kendall, "and I suppose of the thirty or forty we listened to only about two had heard our records, or were the remotest bit interested in the group."[17]

One person who spotted the *Melody Maker* ad and decided to react to it was Birmingham guitarist David J. Ball. Born 30 March 1950, Ball had previously been with former Move bass player Ace Kefford in The Ace Kefford Stand, who released a cover version of The Yardbirds' "For Your Love" (Atlantic 589 260, 1969). Out of the ashes of this group Big Bertha was born, whose only UK single was "The World's An Apple" (Altantic 584 298, 1969).

Dave Ball cites his main influences as Eric Clapton and "basically any old blues player that Eric would mention in interviews". At the time when he saw Procol Harum's advert in *Melody Maker* he wasn't aware of anything the group had recorded since "Homburg". Nevertheless, he managed to get himself an audition with them and, out of the many applicants, he was chosen – according to himself not because of his musical abilities as much as for being able to tell some good jokes.

While not as strong a player as Robin Trower, Dave Ball nevertheless comes across as a very capable guitarist. His style is raw, perhaps more heavy rock than straight blues. At the same time he has a considerably gentler side to his playing, as he demonstrated on Procol Harum's famous 1972 album, *Live In Concert with the Edmonton Symphony Orchestra*.

Soon after Dave Ball had joined it turned out that a roadie, who had recently started working for the group, was also a friend of Matthew Fisher, and through him Fisher was once again approached to join Procol Harum.

Keith Reid (laughing): "Matthew came down and played with us for a couple of days, and then he fucked off. He got five hundred quid and fucked off. He ran off. Yeah, he let us down. He fucked us about."

However, Matthew Fisher claims to have been genuinely interested. The problem was that he had also been offered a job working for CBS which involved moving to the USA and becoming a house producer for the label.

"If I joined Procol again I had to make some financial demands, because if I ditched the offer from CBS I wouldn't have any income at all," he told me. "But I liked the fact that they were now signed to Chrysalis Management; that looked like an improvement. Eventually they gave me £500 as a royalty payment for producing *A Salty Dog*."

The group now started rehearsing to go on tour, their repertoire including a number of songs Matthew Fisher had never played before.

"We didn't do any brand new titles," he recalled. "None of the stuff that later ended up on *Grand Hotel*. But we did rehearse some material from *Home* and *Broken Barricades*. I remember that we played 'Barnyard Story' with me on bass and Chris Copping on organ, which I liked doing. But I had serious doubts about Robin not being in the group any more. It felt as though he had left this great big hole in the band. So after a few days I called Gary and said, 'Look, I don't think that this new guitarist is good enough.' Gary said, 'Come on, give the guy a chance.' I'd say that if the money problem had been more generally sorted and we'd found a better guitarist I would have stayed."

Instead Fisher left the group once again, not to come back until twenty years later. As Dave Ball recalled, "He said he was going to the dentist. So off he went and after that we never saw him again."

Gary Brooker: "We said, '*That* is it!' We called him a rude name and said never, never again."

With less than eight weeks to go before two North American tours and a tour of Europe, Reid and Brooker now had to realise that their plans to find a new organ player were getting nowhere.

"So we decided to take Chris off the bass and put him on the organ full-time," Reid explained, "because when he originally joined us it was with the intention of playing a lot of organ which, through various circumstances, he never had. We said, 'Well, you play organ all the time and we will get another bass player,' which was a much easier thing to do."

B.J. Wilson suggested his old school-friend Alan George Cartwright, whom he had played with in his very first group. Since then Cartwright had for a long while been a member of soul band Freddie Mack's Boss Sound (who briefly featured BJ Wilson on drums). Later he had joined Sweetwater Canal and then Every Which Way, a group led by former Nice drummer Brian Davidson (Cartwright played on their self-titled 1970 LP on Charisma, CAS 1021). Since losing their lead singer, Graham Bell, this group had run into difficulties in finding their own direction and Cartwright quickly agreed to become Procol Harum's new bass player. The others found him a likeable person, quick to learn and very adaptable to the style of the group and to Wilson's playing in particular. His joining meant that Procol Harum were finally up and running again.

After short visits to the USA and Europe the new line-up started out on their main 1971 North American tour.

It was two years since Procol Harum had appeared at the Shakespeare Festival in Stratford, Ontario, Canada where they had performed the song cycle "In Held 'Twas In I" with a symphony orchestra. Now they were once again approached by promoters to visit Canada and play a concert in a somewhat similar setting. However, this time it would be a full performance of Procol Harum material arranged for group and orchestra.

The idea of mixing the two types of musical settings was not entirely new. In fact, augmenting a rock or even a blues band with a string section was by 1971 a tried-and-tested formula. With its occasional classical influences, progressive rock was an obvious target for the idea of elaborating on this formula and truly merge the two musical styles rather than just augment one genre with the instrumentation of the other.

Unfortunately, the few attempts which had been made so far in a "live" setting were less than satisfactory (like for instance Deep Purple's *Concerto For Group And Orchestra*). Quite simply, it is an immense problem to make a symphony orchestra rock and roll.

The combination had worked in the studio for Procol Harum on a couple of the quieter tracks on *A Salty Dog*, but with the Stratford 1969 performance of "In Held 'Twas In I" the band had embarked in a new and extremely daring direction. To all accounts it had worked in Stratford, but one can never tell how much the success of a "live" performance relies on the experience of actually being there. To judge the event more clinically you have to make a recording, and no recording was apparently made of the Stratford 1969 concert.

Furthermore, the material performed has to be carefully selected. As Keith Reid put it to Paul Kendall, "There has got to be an empathy with the music that the group is creating and the kind of music that an orchestra is capable of creating."[18]

When the invitation came to go to Edmonton in Canada and record a concert with the local symphony orchestra and a choir of amateur singers Brooker had already more than half an album's worth of orchestral arrangements written. "In Held 'Twas In I" had been scored in 1969, and so had "A Salty Dog" (though not for a full orchestra, just for a string section). Another song, "All This And More", had appeared with a brass ensemble on the *A Salty Dog* LP.

Apart from these songs the intention was to perform orchestrated versions of "Whaling Stories", "Luskus Delph", "Simple Sister", "Shine On Brightly" and "Repent Walpurgis" (for which producer Chris Thomas had written a score). Finally, the concert would open with Chris Copping and the orchestra playing Albinoni's famous "Adagio".

All these extra songs were in fact performed and recorded on the evening of the concert, but only "Whaling Stories" subsequently survived the mixing stage along with "Luskus Delph" (which became a UK B-side). It is worth noting that initially there was no intention to include "Conquistador", and no orchestral arrangement had been written for the song.

The Edmonton concert was only one out of a long string of commitments in connection with Procol Harum's autumn 1971 North American tour. Hence there was considerable pressure on the group and particularly on Gary Brooker, who in the midst of everything else had to find the time and energy to write the remaining orchestral arrangements:

"What we've always done if Procol recorded a song and I re-orches-trated it, which I did many times – it's almost been like recomposing, writing a lot of other themes to go in with everything else. You've got what the band's playing, you can enhance that with the orchestra and the choir, but at the same time they're all there so you give them something else to do as well. There's quite a lot of difference musical-ly in what's going on in the background between 'Whaling Stories' in the studio and 'Whaling Stories' in Edmonton, and between 'In Held 'Twas In I' from *Shine On Brightly* and the one at Edmonton. I think it always blended well. The orchestra went well with the songs."

It had been arranged that the concert be recorded by Wally Heider's Mobile Unit, who in mid-November 1971 along with the band depart-ed from Los Angeles, their course set for Canada.

"When we were just about to go up there I thought that we needed another fast one," Gary Brooker said. "You can get a bit too orchestral and too 'Salty Doggy' and slow. I thought it just needed something more of a rock song, so I thought of doing 'Conquistador' and I think the introduction and that funny trumpet bit and everything sort of just added that little bit extra to it and the atmosphere of it."

As a consequence Dave Ball recalled "the rest of us sitting on the plane going up there and humming bits and pieces, while Gary was busy writing the parts".

There were a number of other difficulties in connection with the Edmonton concert. "As I recall it, Paul McCartney had been busted not long before," explained Ball, "so there was a problem getting our equipment and everything through customs and we were considerably delayed when we finally managed to get up there."

When Procol Harum eventually got to rehearse with the orchestra it was only a couple of days before the concert. First Gary Brooker had a note rehearsal with the conductor and then later another rehearsal with the choir who, since they were amateurs, were available only at night.

According to Chris Copping the group were half way through rehearsing "A Salty Dog", it was going well and things were finally looking up – then the hour struck and the bassoon player in the orchestra, who appears to have also been the local union representa-tive, stood up announcing, "Thank you, gentlemen. Time. End of rehearsal."

To the astonishment of everyone else, the orchestra walked out. After some negotiation they agreed to come back and do an extra hour of rehearsal, but the arrangers still hadn't managed to get the choir and the orchestra together at the same time. As a result it was impossible to stage the whole performance before the actual event.

On top of all this Dave Ball's amplifier went on strike on the afternoon of the concert, prompting him to go and get another amp from a shop in town. Arriving back at the hall he found that the new amplifier didn't work either, so he had to find a third one. He played it for the first time at the concert itself – luckily this one worked.

The concert didn't begin particularly well. On the Albinoni piece Chris Copping was badly out of timing with the orchestra, and the lead violinist was out of tune. However, the piece was never meant as more than a warm-up.

Now the entire band finally went on stage and after a short introduction from Gary Brooker the orchestra burst into the brand-new arrangement for "Conquistador".

Right from the start drama and dynamics became the key words for the event, and a warm sympathy seems to have been present between all involved. For a moment, however, it was close to falling apart during the first song. Dave Ball burst into a brilliant distorted mayhem of blues-inspired phrases – so brilliant, in fact, that he felt no enticement to stop.

"I was playing all I could," he recalled. "I was totally into my solo, so I didn't notice that it had actually ended. There I was, still playing on, though I suppose the audience didn't hear it 'cause the engineer has probably turned the sound off. Finally, I came to what I thought was the end of my solo and to my amazement I found that everyone around me had long since gone back into the next verse. I can just imagine the audience staring at each other and thinking there's something pretty strange going on. Just me getting carried away, you know."

Part of Ball's problem could have been that the sound balance on stage was very poor indeed. Furthermore the band, apart from Brooker and Copping (who were positioned on each side of the stage facing each other), couldn't see the orchestra, choir or conductor, who were all standing behind them.

The role of the orchestra was primarily to vary the colouration of the group's sound (the only place where Brooker felt tempted to enhance the basic structure of a song was during the introduction and middle bridge of "Conquistador", which only lasts for a few bars). Nevertheless, these subtle, tasteful arrangements provided a dramatic change in the entire mood of the music.

If the impression you get from listening to Procol Harum recordings up until this point is best compared with "viewing a crackled old oil painting hanging in the corner of some dimly lit cathedral", then Brooker changed that altogether with his orchestral arrangements on the *Live* album. By painting in pastels and brighter colours and bringing the calm and beauty of an English summer landscape into his personal idiom, the result was far more *Wind In The Willows* than *The Trial*. The question is, of course, whether or not this is coherent with Reid's lyrics and their dark subject matter. Personally, I think the project is extremely successful and not in the least illogical. Since Reid's lyrics – particularly those chosen for this "live" performance – are so obviously concerned with classic human mysteries, there is somewhere in the equation a longing for redemption and the anticipation of an existence "beyond these things" where pastoral beauty prevails. This is exactly what Brooker brings to the fore via his orchestral scores.

It goes without saying that, in order to make room for no less than a symphony orchestra and a choir in a soundscape as densely occupied as Procol Harum's, the role of the instruments in the original line-up must be diminished. Consequently, organ and piano were featured far less prominently, while the drumming became even more percussion based than before, the bass guitar acting primarily as an addition to the bass drum.

Dave Ball's guitar remained an important feature, but it was far less penetrating than Robin Trower's playing had ever been, enabling it to blend better with the orchestra and choir. Furthermore, on "All This And More" Ball used a pleasant finger style which has more in common with Renaissance lute playing than with modern rock guitar.

Coming backstage after the final number, satisfied with their performance and with the audience still clapping furiously back in the hall, the group were met by a frantic-looking Chris Thomas and a debate immediately ensued between him and Gary Brooker concerning what the group needed to go out and do again.

Finally, the band went out to perform their encore, "Repent Walpurgis", after which Brooker explained to the audience that since a recording was being made tonight there were a few things which needed to be done again. Would they mind staying in their seats while the people on stage had another go at some of the songs?

The question was answered by more applause. The concert continued and eventually ended with a standing ovation - a positive antidote to all the turmoil the band had been through.

For some the troubles were all over now; for others they were just beginning. Chris Copping recalled hearing parts of the concert shortly after the event and being horrified - "It sounded a mess on the multi-track!" Apparently, the mixing and editing would be a tough job.

Procol Harum Live In Concert With The Edmonton Symphony Orchestra was released in May 1972. It became a well-deserved success both on the critical front and on the sales front, reaching the Top 5 in the USA.

In retrospect it seems no wonder that the album did so well. However, at the time it came as a big surprise to the group themselves.

"I was completely unaware that the album had started to sell," said Chris Copping. "Normally your record company will tell you when something like that happens. But I was reading the *Melody Maker* one day and I saw that the album had reached number 13 in the US charts. I was quite taken aback. Then of course it just continued to climb upwards from there."

The album also spawned the first real hit single Procol Harum had enjoyed since 1967, ironically with a song written back in that same year, "Conquistador".

The success of the single further helped album sales and, in addition to this, touring had been organised to coincide with the release of the LP. It was just entering the US Top 20 when the group arrived in America to find themselves selling out places they had never played before. Incidentally, the warm-up group on that tour was a then up-and-coming band called The Eagles.

Returning to England Procol Harum started work on their new studio album, *Grand Hotel*. Gary Brooker had written a fresh set of songs to a handful of Keith Reid lyrics which were less sombre and morbid than most of his previous output. However, with this album the grandiosity of the band's music would be taken to a new and perhaps not entirely healthy extreme.

Halfway through the recordings Dave Ball suddenly announced his departure.

"It was all down to my dissatisfaction with what I was doing," he told Bob Lloyd, "my inability to stay in anything too long without getting depressed by the whole affair, and the fact that I was very unused to playing the same thing over and over again. There were also some very, very slight personal differences that seemed to creep into the politics of the band between myself and BJ. Though it didn't affect us more than a day – in Kansas – after that it seemed to make a difference to the evenness of the band. Just things weren't sitting right. I think I probably pre-empted things by just upping and leaving, but I don't know. I tried to get a straight answer when I left. It was right in the middle of *Grand Hotel*, it wasn't an auspicious time to leave."

Part Five

Deaths and rebirths, 1972-1999

Going down slow

Keith always said it should be this and it should be that. It was that way right until the end. That was one of the real strong points of the group. It was very much in the control of somebody who had an idea. When you don't have that with the best of bands it can float all over the place and you never get anything solid.

BJ Wilson

Mick Grabham wasn't exactly a newcomer to the music scene when he joined Procol Harum in the autumn of 1972. As a teenager in the mid-sixties he had been in a variety of local bands in North East England, after which he moved south to join the newly-started Plastic Penny who had recently had a hit with "Everything I Am". When this group folded after three LP releases Grabham formed the West Coast influenced rock band Cochise, with whom he made three more albums between 1970 and 1972.

Following the demise of this band he and ex-Spencer Davis Group guitarist Ray Fenwick founded the innovative but ill-fated Guitar Orchestra, whose 1971 album wasn't released until some twenty-five years later. Grabham also rubbed shoulders with songwriters Dave Elliott and Emitt Rhodes, who were both influences on his own brief solo career.

In fact, this career amounted to no more than one LP and a single. To ardent Procol Harum fans the original *Mick The Lad* album has long been an attractive collector's item, and it is easy enough to see why, since listening to it opens up a new understanding of the group in their later phases. Sadly, it also reveals a vast potential of talent and ideas inside the band that were never fully explored. There certainly were not many multi-tracked guitar solos, gently flowing chord progressions, or elaborate vocal harmony arrangements on mid-seventies Procol Harum records. However, the tougher R&B approach, so brilliantly displayed on the bonus tracks gracing the compact disc issue of *Mick The Lad*, can perhaps be recognised as an influence on Harum's shifting into a higher gear on their 1974 album, *Exotic Birds And Fruit*.

Unlike Dave Ball, Mick Grabham had for years been a keen Procol Harum fan and followed the group's career closely. In the summer of 1971, when the band were looking for a guitarist after Trower's departure, Grabham had tried to get an audition but was informed by the group's management that he was too late – by then Dave Ball had already been given the job. However, the following year Grabham was successful.

Mick Grabham's arrival signalled a new era in Procol Harum's history with much more stability. Unfortunately, it also coincided with a general creative crisis within the British rock scene, starting around the end of 1972. Most of the bigger surviving names from the sixties were clearly losing touch with their roots and the truly interesting new music no longer came from the rock department of popular music; it had instead quietly shifted over to the folk revival scene.

Mind you, at the time a lot of it seemed quite good. Procol Harum's 1973 effort, *Grand Hotel*, certainly sounded fine to this boy's ears. I was fifteen and went from being aware of the group, and knowing a few of their more commercial successes, to becoming an ardent, longstanding follower.

One of the many advantages Procol Harum had over other bands was that I could play their music in my family's living room without my parents shouting for me to be quiet. And by "play" I don't mean just spin the records but also get hold of the sheet music and actually knock it out on Granny's old piano standing over in the corner. If I closed my eyes I could dream for a moment that I was Gary Brooker – though repeated attempts to "hit those high notes" quickly brought me back to cold reality.

Grand Hotel meant a shift in Procol Harum's main audience from the USA to Continental Europe. Living in Denmark at the time I can confirm the impact it had, and not just on my own generation. As most of the teachers at the Copenhagen college I attended were only in their early thirties or younger, they too were very aware of the band and obviously bought their records and appreciated their music. There was no generation gap there to worry about. In fact, our music teachers played these records to us and analyzed them with us.

So it was natural when some of us started getting bands together in the music room after school hours that it would be titles from the Procol Harum songbook we mainly had a stab at. I was eighteen myself when we did our first concert in the school hall before a large audience of parents, pupils and teachers, performing "A Salty Dog" and "Grand Finale" augmented by the school choir. Shortly afterwards we visited another college, and their band played the entire *Grand Hotel* album – dressed in top hats and tail coats!

One thing I've often noticed, even before immigrating to Britain in 1992, is that the importance Procol Harum had for youngsters like us all around Europe at the time completely eluded most people here, where the mention of the group to this day more often than not causes outbursts like, "Oh yeah, great group, I really love 'Nights In White Satin' in particular." Sorry mate, wrong ship.

But before getting all nostalgic I have to admit that listening to most of Harum's later output brings me considerably less pleasure today than it did at the time. Of their last four albums only *Exotic Birds And Fruit* still sounds wholesome, fresh and artistically successful throughout, while I find *Grand Hotel* in particular pretty much a cold execution.

Nevertheless, even that album has its moments. Songs like "Toujours l'Amour", "Bringing Home The Bacon" and "A Rum Tale" are Brooker-Reid classics, while newcomer Mick Grabham's solo guitar playing is overwhelming. The fact that he was brought in at a very late stage during the proceedings and on most songs had to put his guitar on top of already-recorded tracks further emphasises his talents and his ability to fit in with the group.

In fact, Grabham's arrival came so late that all the photographs for the sleeve had already been shot with Dave Ball in the line-up. To have new pictures taken apparently went beyond the budget Chrysalis had set for the LP, so instead Dave Ball was crudely beheaded and pictures of Mick Grabham's bearded face were glued on instead. A swift way to gain a couple of inches in height! The only picture in which Ball still appears is the distorted image inside the tall-stemmed glass on the back of the sleeve. Likewise, the only guitar work of his which remained on the record was some acoustic strumming on "Souvenir Of London".

As Procol Harum's latest addition Mick Grabham was thrown in at the deep end. The first gig he ever played with the band was a concert with the Royal Philharmonic Orchestra. During the following year the group also played with orchestras in both Europe and the USA. A concert in California with the Los Angeles Philharmonic Orchestra was recorded and released as a radio station promo in the US. Unfortunately, it is by no means as impressive as the Edmonton concert, and Grabham in particular sounds uncomfortable.

In the studio, because of his ability to go along with the group's established ideas, Mick Grabham has generally been seen as the perfect choice for the band. Most notably, he was able to play amazing solos over difficult chord changes, something Robin Trower had never been keen to do. On the *Grand Hotel* album, in particular, Grabham's solos are carefully rehearsed while still very bluesy and retaining a margin for improvisation.

However, when he tried to cut loose on stage and be more of a blues guitarist he would run into exactly the same problems as both Trower and Ball had struggled with. Judging from the times I saw him myself, and from listening to some of the many bootleg concert recordings made with Grabham in the band, I would say that it sounds as though he now and again found himself playing notes that did not fit the unusual chord structures. Or, he would find that his solo was already over and the band were way into the next verse of the song (much as Dave Ball describes playing on "Conquistador" at the Edmonton concert). Robin Trower at least had the authority either to just keep on playing with such conviction that it didn't matter if things were formally right or wrong, or he would simply refuse to play on certain songs.

Mick Grabham has described his role in Procol Harum as that of a "yes man", and on several occasions I have found him somewhat frustrated with his own career and the way things went. I can see why. I personally think that if anyone suffered from the decline of Procol Harum during their final years, it is Mick Grabham. He had the potential to be a much bigger name, but he got stuck on board the Harum ship, and when it sank the chance to become a more widely-known and appreciated artist had already passed him by.

"I still have a great affection for Gary, greater than for anyone else involved probably," Grabham told me in my first interview with him in the early eighties. "It's always just disappointed me that his R&B influence wasn't utilised as much as it should have been. It was just the way things had gone. It had become more of a business thing. It hadn't consciously, nobody phoned everybody up saying, 'Right, we're having a business meeting,' and all this. But the business side of things had taken over, really, compared to the music. Not that I'm saying Gary put that first and foremost, he wouldn't, he'd put the music first and foremost, but in fact the way it came out it was all lots of dealings... Suddenly it's like the business side of it takes over to a degree and for my money I'd rather have spent that energy on the music."

Like Robin Trower, Grabham is first and foremost a rhythm 'n' blues guitarist. When the rare occasion came and he could finally go his own way and do what he did best, he would prove himself an even better guitarist than anyone had dared to imagine.

It didn't happen very often but one occasion was the 1975 concert for the closing-down of London's Rainbow Theatre where Procol Harum backed singer Frankie Miller on a selection of mainly standard rhythm 'n' blues songs. Only two tracks from this concert made it on to vinyl, "Brickyard Blues", and a version of "Grand Hotel" with Brooker singing lead. Unfortunately, neither of these songs is as powerful a performance as those which got left out: "Devil Gun", "If You Need Me", "Train" and "He'll Have To Go".

Hopefully these tracks – along with many, many other high quality unreleased Procol Harum "live" and studio recordings – will one day see the light of day as an official release. They deserve it, and to my mind the thousands of fans all over the world who for decades have faithfully supported Procol Harum deserve to hear them. It certainly makes more sense than letting the magnetic tapes rot away on a shelf somewhere.

Going back to *Grand Hotel*, it seemed that Keith Reid had progressed in some ways and become more professional and aware of contemporary trends, but as I see it there are only few occasions where he comes anywhere near the intensity, urgency and originality of his earlier efforts. The most important thing, however, was that he could still inspire Gary Brooker to write fine music.

While *Grand Hotel* in many ways was a true seventies album (more mannerism than music), *Exotic Birds And Fruit* marked a return to form and remains the group's finest effort from their later years. In the dull climate that was British pop at the time Procol Harum took the only decent route and became more of a straightforward rock band than they'd ever been before.

Gary Brooker remembered that, "We made the 'live' album with an orchestra. We'd then taken an orchestra into the studio on *Grand Hotel* and did a lot of work with that in easier surroundings – we could work on it for a week instead of only one night. But I think after *Grand Hotel* and a few concerts we did, we said we'd had enough of orchestras. Let's get back and just be a band again."

The album opener, "Nothing But The Truth", is a great song built on a hefty Motown beat set to a series of ascending bass lines and baroque chord sequences. The music for "Beyond The Pale" has a surprisingly Jewish atmosphere (particularly since the lyric is supposed to be about touring in Iceland), while "Strong As Samson" is more Dylan-esque and could probably under the right circumstances have been a hit.

"The Idol" features some fine guitar soloing, while the first song on side two – "The Thin End Of The Wedge" – manages to be different from anything else the group ever wrote, based on strange, unison scales but nevertheless catchy; one of the most intriguing songs Brooker-Reid have written.

"Butterfly Boys" (reputedly a criticism of the band's record label who used a butterfly logo) and "Monsieur R. Monde" (a then-unreleased 1967 song revisited) are both fine rockers. "Fresh Fruit" is a bit of an oddball and perhaps not as funny as it was meant to be, but the overall mood is rounded off in the best of taste with "New Lamps For Old".

The album spawned one single at the time with "Nothing But The Truth", backed by a non-album cut called "Drunk Again" (apparently not a totally inapt description of the group on tour at this stage).

For 1974 this LP was a revelation; I for one could hardly believe my ears when it started to come out on the radio. It sold well in mainland Europe, but on the whole it didn't do much commercially compared with the group's larger successes, despite some decent reviews.

Some criticism has been raised over Chris Thomas's production work on Procol Harum's records, which after the *Live* LP was rather polished and involved a large amount of reverb (very unusual for the time). In fact, on *Exotic Birds And Fruit* it sounds as if the group is playing to an empty hall - probably not the best of images to promote.

"We were starting to scratch around a bit," Gary Brooker recalled. "What happened after *Exotic Birds* – we enjoyed the album and liked it, but it came around again that it was time to go into studios. We had made three or four albums in AIR Studios with Chris Thomas and the same engineer at the same time of year, and there we were again, about to go into the same situation, and we suddenly said, 'Let's do something else. What do we wanna do?'"

As the plan was to get increasingly R&B influenced, that naturally formed the basis of the band's search for a new producer. It then emerged that Mike Leiber and Jerry Stoller, the famous songwriting duo who in the fifties had created big hits for, among others, The Coasters and Elvis Presley, were in Britain working on an album for Stealers Wheel.

"We thought that they could be good for us," said Brooker, "'cause we liked them as producers, and we hoped that they would be able to perhaps help us interpret our songs with their influence a bit. In fact, we sent them our songs that we had, and they said, 'We'd love to do it'. So that was that. So we got a different studio. We went to The Who's studio."

In fact working with Leiber & Stoller turned out to be quite different from what Procol Harum had expected.

"They would come in and play us one of their songs," Brooker continued. "New ones, in a bit of a strange style. We said, 'Why don't we do "Baby I Don't Care",' and we did 'Baby I Don't Care' which they wrote. They'd go, 'Ooh, great version – but how about this one we've just written?' And then they'd play another one. We said, 'What about *our* stuff?' It was like that all the time. In the end we did 'I Keep Forgetting'. That was a compromise 'cause it was one of their songs so they'd earn a little bit more money, and we liked it."

A result of this situation was that some rather strange material ended up on the ensuing album, titled *Procol's Ninth*. Lennon and McCartney's "Eight Days A Week" in particular sounds weak. Luckily, other tracks are more successfully executed, and the album also includes a fine attempt to mix Procol Harum with a horn section, something the band hadn't incorporated since "Playmate Of The Mouth" on *Broken Barricades*.

The horns work particularly well on "I Keep Forgetting", the old Leiber & Stoller composition, which is delivered with all the desperation it deserves, a truly fantastic vocal performance. Nevertheless, it is strange suddenly to find songs on a Procol Harum LP which are not written by Brooker-Reid. And even some of their own material sounds slightly unfinished. "The Piper's Tune", for instance, introduces a Scottish mood and appears to be yelling out for bagpipes to be added.

Gary Brooker: "Try telling Leiber and Stoller that. There's gotta be, hasn't there? I mean, we're almost playing the pipes, we're sort of putting that sound in. There were a few doubtfuls on that album, even from our point of view, particularly 'Eight Days A Week'. I don't know *how* that got on there. But I think we got a great single out of it, 'Pandora's Box'. I think that was the best track on there."

"Pandora's Box" was yet another left-over from the earliest days of the group. It had been recorded in 1967 but never released. Leiber & Stoller added a catchy marimba riff to the arrangement, after which the group re-recorded the song.

Keith Reid: "They made that song into a hit. It was a song that we always really liked but somehow it didn't seem to come off. And when we did it with them it came off really well. They put the flute solo on... in some ways they were very good."

"I was beginning to get a little bit worried by now, actually," recalled Brooker, "because in 1967 I wrote 'A Whiter Shade Of Pale' and I also wrote 'Homburg'. Then in 1967 I also wrote 'Conquistador', which was a hit in 1972. And in 1967 I also wrote 'Pandora's Box' which was a hit in 1975. I thought, 'Is that my whole sum of hits, all written back then?'"

Can't see much point in carrying on

The rock music scene in 1975/76 was in a pretty dismal state ... With
a few notable exceptions rock 'n' roll seemed to have finally "grown
up" in the worst possible sense.

Bernie Tormé [19]

"Pandora's Box" got to number 16 in the UK charts during June 1975.
In August the album reached its peak position at number 41. It wasn't
exactly "A Whiter Shade Of Pale" all over again, but it could nevertheless have been an appropriate exit for the band, whose days seemed
numbered anyway. Instead they carried on for another two years, writing, recording, and above all touring.

Mick Grabham: "There was at least one tour of Europe a year, that's
if there wasn't an additional couple of weeks here or there in different
parts of Europe. The States were at least once a year too, and then
came all the weirder places like Poland, Iceland, even Mexico."

Though Procol Harum somehow seemed to be in a world of their
own, doing whatever they felt was right for them, there were also
signs of change in the group's style and approach. Perhaps influenced
by the popularity of pub rock around 1976 some gigs would start to
lean much harder on standard rock 'n' roll material. It didn't go down
well. Fans were puzzled, and one particular critic complained that
he'd come to see Procol Harum, not a revamped version of some
ghastly, long-forgotten sixties group called The Paramounts!

Other bands tried the same formula of returning to R&B roots in order to keep up with changing trends, perhaps most notably Gentle Giant. It didn't pay off for them either. Others again, like Genesis, went in another direction and chose to become much more pop and chart-orientated – that worked and would probably have been the only way Procol Harum could have salvaged their career. Instead they went and did probably the worst thing anyone could have done by 1977—they released a weedy progressive rock album.

Gary Brooker recalls, "Again we thought, 'Okay, let's have a plan, what shall we do this time?' We were gonna produce ourselves with the help of some engineers in Criterion Studios, so everything's gonna go smoothly 'cause it's Americans. So we went over to Miami where we got involved with two guys there."

The "two guys" were brothers Ron and Howie Albert, who during the late seventies were much-in-demand US producers and engineers. It was a long time since Procol Harum had last recorded an album, so they had quite a lot of new material, at least fourteen songs. To present them to the Albert brothers all these tracks were performed and recorded during one long session. Since quite a few of the songs didn't go on the final album and haven't been released in any other form either, it seems worth going through them in detail:

THE MIAMI 1976 SESSION
I'm A Reader And A Writer
An up-tempo rocker with rhythmic changes and lots of solo guitar. Unreleased. Played "live" during 1976-77.
A La Carte
Jazzy R&B, reminiscent of Georgie Fame in the mid-sixties. Unreleased.
So Far Behind
A 1967 song revisited. Slow, beautiful Brooker-Reid organ drenched classic. Played during mid-seventies in an up-tempo arrangement. Unreleased.
Fish Dinner For Two
Tongue-in-cheek 1930s pastiche, a bit like The Beatles' "Your Mother Should Know". Unreleased.
Mark Of The Claw
Rawer, more exciting than the LP version.

Strangers In Space
Livelier, less sleep-inducing than album version.
Backgammon
A more shambolic version of this pointless instrumental, which ended up on the B-side of the "Wizard Man" single.
Wizard Man
Less polished, looser than the official release.
Musical Fish
A waltz somewhat in the same vein as "A Rum Tale". Unreleased.
Something Magic
Dry, more basic rendition than on the LP. Middle bridge chaotic.
One Eye On The Future
Organ fuelled old-style Harum perfection. Played "live" 1977. Unreleased.
Skating On Thin Ice
Another album track. No strings on this version.
Old Dog
Great shit-kicking country tune with dominant fiddle work. Played "live" 1977 and again at the Redhill party, 1997. Unreleased.
You Better Wait
Another slow, organ based old-style Procol Harum song which could have been a classic. Totally convincing, very moving. Played at least once in concert. Unreleased.

Listening to these legendary sessions at Gary Brooker's home studio back in the eighties there was no doubt in my mind that Procol Harum in 1976 had the potential to make one last, very impressive record. At least three songs – "So Far Behind", "One Eye On The Future" and "You Better Wait" – are quite simply among the finest Brooker-Reid have ever written. However, two things spoiled it for them.

One was the inclusion of a new band member, Pete Solley. Since some of the criticism against the band, both internally and in the music papers, was aimed at the rhythm section's inability to provide a funky, danceable beat, it was decided that some kind of personnel change was needed.

Mick Grabham: "Although Chris was now on organ I heard him play bass again and I though he was a better bass player than Alan Cartwright. So there was some sort of meeting and Alan went and

Chris went on to bass. So we needed an organ player, basically, so we auditioned organ players and Pete Solley got the job."

The idea seemed worth a try. Copping was a much more outward-going player than Alan Cartwright, and Pete Solley was an excellent keyboard player who also played a mean country fiddle on the side. He already had some faint connections with Procol Harum, since he had for several years been a member of the Little Feat-inspired group Snafu, a fine band who also featured Procol Harum's ex-drummer Bobby Harrison as lead vocalist. Solley's Hammond work with this group was particularly impressive. He is obviously a highly talented musician and, according to Matthew Fisher, the only person ever to have sussed 100 percent how to play the organ part on "A Whiter Shade Of Pale".

Unfortunately, Pete Solley for some reason had ditched his Hammond by the time he joined Procol Harum. Instead he used both on stage and in the studio a dreadful, hollow-sounding electronic Farfisa organ and on top of that a few ghastly synthesisers. It not only spoiled the group's entire sound, it was also a very bad commercial choice in 1976/77 when there was a general reaction against the use of such keyboard instruments.

The second problem was that the Albert brothers were far from impressed with the material presented to them.

Gary Brooker remembered that, "What they more or less said was [putting on Richard Nixon accent], 'Look, we don't like 'em. You want us to make an album, you want us to help?' In fact I can give you the exact quote. He said, 'You can take a dog shit, you can cover it with chocolate. But when you bite into it, what have you got? Dog shit!' And this was our first day there to make a new album!

"Well, things really went from bad to worse. I think we ended up doing three or four of the songs that we'd taken over with us and I also had a theme which we'd half-attempted a couple of years before, just a few ideas for some words that Keith had done called 'The Worm And The Tree'. And they said it seemed a good idea. So we kind of recorded it and made it up as we went along, and then I did the orchestration for it. Never did get a chance to work out the tune, so we just spoke it [laughs].

"And that was it, really, it was full circle. It was made in an absolute rush because what we'd imagined we'd be doing when we went there to make this album, we didn't do at all. We ended up doing something which we did not intend to do, really. And the words also on 'The Worm And The Tree' seemed to sound the bell – 'From the ashes', you know – Procol killed itself almost, committed suicide without us even knowing it."

I recall hearing a track from *Something Magic* for the first time with a group of friends. I was doing my National Service at the time and we were downstairs in the basement cleaning some kind of antiquated murder weapons. Most of us were ready to go back upstairs when the DJ on the transistor radio announced a new Procol Harum song called "Strangers In Space".

The music started and we looked at each other in disbelief. After a few moments I found myself alone in the room, still listening and thinking, "There must be something in it. If I buy the record and listen to it some more." But there wasn't. Procol Harum had let me down. Shortly after, their Copenhagen concert that year was cancelled.

Luckily, *Something Magic* sounds better today when you don't tend to compare it so much with what else was happening at the time. "Skating On Thin Ice" has a fine orchestral arrangement by Chris Copping; "Wizard Man" (which wasn't included until the last minute – test pressings and some German copies don't have it) is built on an ear-catching three-chord riff and could have come from the repertoire of The Rumours. More songs in this vein might have done the group some good.

However, Keith Reid's peculiar attempt to write a simple and straightforward story about trees and worms and noble young men – the much dreaded "The Worm And The Tree" which takes up the entire side two – ought never to have seen the light of day. Brooker's orchestral arrangements are impeccable as always, but otherwise this long track comes across as a mixture of the worst material on *Grand Hotel*, a third division progressive act (something like Fruupp), and Terry Wogan narrating *Peter And The Wolf*. No wonder audiences were booing at gigs, and the group started looking increasingly miserable in photographs.

Furthermore, as a band they continued to crack up during these last few months of their existence, partly because of personal dissatisfaction among certain members, partly because of yet another change in the line-up.

"When I joined them I was absolutely ecstatic," recalled Mick Grabham. "To join a band that you've always admired like that – it was an absolute gift. But to a degree at the beginning I was completely overawed by it, by me luck, really. Consequently, in that kind of a situation you're a 'yes man'. I just went along with whatever. Then slowly and surely as things become more normalised and everyone's more accustomised and it's a regular thing you don't want to be a bloody 'yes man' any longer. You want to contribute something yourself without being told. I'm not saying I was trying to stamp my personality all over it, I was just trying to keep some enthusiasm going!"

Some of the dissatisfaction was aimed at Chris Copping in particular.

"I got the elbow," Chris Copping admitted in Bob Lloyd's interview. "I was asked to leave, but I was being a silly boy anyway. There's no real hostility about it, because the band kind of faded after that anyway. I think they were really kind to me, because the band made a loss on that last tour."

Instead the late Dee Murray was brought in for this tour only. He was an old friend of Mick Grabham and primarily known as a longstanding member of Elton John's Band – an extremely professional player whose expertise is underlined by the fact that the group rehearsed with him for only two days before going out on tour.

This situation in particular seems to have caused animosity between Mick Grabham and BJ Wilson, who from the outset had been displeased with seeing his old school pal Alan Cartwright leaving because of complaints from the guitarist. Now it was Grabham's old pal playing bass instead...

"Getting Dee Murray into the group was like getting in the fucking London Symphony Orchestra," BJ Wilson told me. "Totally out of proportion."

In the spring of 1977 the group set out for their last tour of America.

Tired and depressed, exhausted, the members of Procol Harum lie scattered here and there in the chairs behind the stage. It is May 1977 at New York City's Academy of Music. Their undisputed leader through all the years, Gary Brooker, looks around. "This is our last gig," he sighs.

163

No one has spoken about it before, but there is that kind of an atmosphere. No animosity between any of the players tonight, just a feeling that this is their last date. For the last few months the writing has been on the wall. Their tenth and latest LP has in every sense been a fiasco. Audiences are failing them, health is failing too.

Brooker is struggling with a nagging back pain.

Only afterwards does he realise that it is almost to the day the tenth anniversary of the release of the group's first single, the hit above all hits – "A Whiter Shade Of Pale".

And so it was that later

You often find that people who break new ground do it alone and it's not recognised at the time that you've done it.

Robin Trower

This final chapter contains brief descriptions of the post-Procol Harum activities of Gary Brooker, Robin Trower, Matthew Fisher and other group members, plus the 1990s Procol Harum reunion.

Gary Brooker

After the break-up of Procol Harum in May 1977 it was expected that Gary Brooker would immediately try to launch a solo career. It didn't quite happen like that. Instead, he found that he had a lot of catching up to do in matters that had little to do with music.

"I'd never had a chance to go fishing, I'd never had a chance to plant my vegetables or look after the chickens, silly little things. And also, I don't know what I did but I injured myself somewhere in the last tour and I had a problem with my back.

"It was just as well that Procol ended because I got into a great deal of pain over the next year where I couldn't concentrate at all, I couldn't sit down at the piano, I couldn't stand up at the piano, I couldn't listen to a record or anything. So the period lent itself quite well, really. I did a few things that I hadn't done before – I went on holiday and just messed around at home and got over this injury."

Yet, little by little music inevitably found its way back into Brooker's life. He discovered that he couldn't keep away from it, so he started turning the barn on his property in Surrey into a private rehearsal- and demo-studio.

Soon afterwards came the making of his first solo album, *(No More) Fear Of Flying* (May 1979), which finally saw Brooker working with The Beatles' famous producer, George Martin.

"I just wanted to go into the studio and just sing some songs and not, you know, not Procol songs. Not Keith's words, if you like, not even my own songs... Then I joined up with Clapton's band, which I was with for two and a half years. During that time I made a new album as well."

Lead Me To The Water (1982) was an attempt to combine Gary Brooker's old interest in music with a new hobby he had adopted – angling. The LP was recorded with a group of the finest players in British rock – George Harrison, Phil Collins and Eric Clapton.

In 1983 Brooker re-established contact with Matthew Fisher, and together with Keith Reid they wrote most of the songs for *Echoes In The Night* (1985), which also featured BJ Wilson. It was a fine contemporary-sounding LP but probably not quite what die-hard Procol Harum fans had been hoping for.

Brooker now entered the second phase of his life where music had to take a back seat to other activities. He bought a pub in Surrey called The Parrot, and he was also doing more and more fishing. So much, in fact, that in 1987 he became Fly Fishing Champion of Europe.

Music was still on the agenda, but mainly as a spare-time activity in his own pub and on the charity front. Brooker formed No Stiletto Shoes, an R&B group, with ex-Amen Corner frontman Andy Fairweather-Low on guitar and an otherwise somewhat fluid line-up.

In 1990 the Royal Theatre in Copenhagen invited him to write the music for a ballet. The piece was entitled *Delta* and premiered on December 20 the same year.

The following year Procol Harum were finally reformed.

Robin Trower

Robin Trower's first attempt to get a group together after leaving Procol Harum in 1971 came with the formation of Jude, a line-up which included James Dewar on bass and backing vocals (ex-The

Luvvers and Stone The Crows), drummer Clive Bunker (ex-Jethro Tull) and lead singer Frankie Miller, whom Trower had initially got together with just to write songs.

Robin Trower recalls, "It was a good idea but it didn't work. So I went on from there and while I was in that band I'd decided that Jimmy had a really good voice and I still wanted to have a three-piece, so I asked Jimmy to join me as a singer."

Reg Isadore (ex-Quiver) was auditioned and turned out to be the right man for the job. The band, simply calling themselves Robin Trower, rehearsed for a long while and then made some demo recordings.

"Nobody was interested, but eventually Chrysalis said that they would put it out in the hope that they would sell enough to pay the cost just on the strength of me being in Procol Harum. Little did they realise that it was going to be this monstrous big thing."

Next Matthew Fisher was invited to produce the group's first record.

"Matthew did a very good job," Trower recalled, "but I also think Geoff Emerick, the engineer, played a big part in the success of our second album, *Bridge Of Sighs*. That was the first successful album."

After *Bridge Of Sighs*, a Platinum LP in the USA, Reg Isadore was replaced by former Sly and the Family Stone drummer, Bill Lordan.

The immense success of Trower's new group was almost entirely based in the USA. In Britain he was more-or-less written off as a Jimi Hendrix copyist (his band's highest position came in 1976, when *Robin Trower Live* reached No. 15 in the album charts).

"I was the very first to come along sounding like I had been pinching from Hendrix," Trower told me, "but I think what a lot of people miss is that although I was influenced by Hendrix I was also influenced by everybody who influenced him."

Towards the end of the decade Robin Trower's commercial success had started to wane but he still kept on making highly influential albums. Particularly *In City Dreams* from 1977 seems to have been an important inspiration to a lot of other guitar players.

By now the group had been augmented with bass player Rusty Allen (another ex-Sly and the Family Stone member), allowing James Dewar to concentrate fully on his singing on this album and the following, *Caravan To Midnight*. In 1980 *Victims Of The Fury* was released, which saw Dewar back on bass and Robin Trower for the first time in almost ten years writing with Keith Reid.

Robin Trower's collaboration with Keith Reid around this time continued over the following two albums, where James Dewar's role was taken over by ex-Cream bassist Jack Bruce. While a better "replacement" could hardly have been found, some of the magic had gone out of the group and it was only briefly revisited on 1983's *Back It Up*, which saw Dewar back on vocals.

After that album Jimmy Dewar left Robin Trower for good and the band entered their "wilderness years" during the 1980s. For a while, bassist Dave Bronze was singing lead vocals until this role was taken over by former Gamma member, Davey Pattison. *Take What You Need* from 1988 signalled a change for the better. However, Robin Trower's career was commercially far removed from its former glories when, in 1991, he was invited to become part of the Procol Harum reunion.

Matthew Fisher

Matthew Fisher's involvement on Robin Trower's first three albums has so far marked the commercial peak of his work as a producer. Parallel to this, he also started his own career as a solo artist.

In fact, an earlier attempt at launching such a career had already been made back in 1970, when Fisher signed a contract with A&M to record an album in his own name. Work commenced using top-notch players such as drummer Clem Cattini and bass player Klaus Voormann. Tony Visconti also played bass on a few tracks. Matthew Fisher describes the style on these recordings as being pretty much the same as on his other solo albums later on, but this initial project didn't come off.

"I felt I was taking on too many tasks," he explained. "I particularly had a problem with the lyrics, so eventually it was all scrapped."

In 1971-72 Fisher lived in New York, where he worked as an in-house producer for CBS. On his return to England he rekindled his plans to make a solo LP. Around the same time he was approached by Robin Trower to become his producer.

Matthew Fisher's first solo album, *Journey's End*, was released by RCA in 1973. It was a surprisingly pop-orientated album for an ex-member of Procol Harum. Anyone expecting tracks like "Repent Walpurgis" or "In The Autumn Of My Madness" must have been greatly surprised on its release; nevertheless, it is an excellent collection of songs.

The year after, *Journey's End* was followed up by *I'll Be There*, a rougher production and a sporadically more rocking album. Less consistent than its predecessor, the album nevertheless contained a handful of songs which could have been classics, particularly "She Knows Me" and "Cold Harbour Lane". The record had a certain John Lennon-esque sparseness and bitterness to it; however, failing sales more-or-less established Matthew Fisher as an acquired taste with record buying audiences.

During the late seventies Fisher spent most of his energy setting up his own studio, Old Barn Recorders, in his native Croydon. One of several interesting projects embarked upon at this time was a solo album by Robin Trower's lead singer James Dewar. As the project went along it evolved into a close collaboration between Dewar and Fisher, both as writers and musicians. If anyone had ever felt that Matthew Fisher's musical ideas had previously been let down by his own vocal delivery, this was very good news indeed.

The James Dewar LP was titled *Stumbledown Romancer* and is an excellent record which combines the talents of Matthew Fisher with a much more up-front vocal performance. Unfortunately, the album never got released at the time. Instead it came out on CD in 1998 (Chrysalis 93153 2) as an indication of what might have been. A more established Dewar-Fisher Band could have come a long way. (Unfortunately, James Dewar is today very ill and no longer active on the musical front.)

In 1981 Fisher released his own fourth album, called *Strange Days*. It was very much a departure from past endeavours. Gone were the big arrangements, the orchestras, even the Hammond. Instead there were synths, drum tapes and so on. Matthew Fisher had fallen for Gary Numan's approach to the new wave. It would take some time for the die-hard fans to come to terms with this album, but the songs and the singing were perhaps Fisher's best ever, and a writing collaboration with Chris White (ex-The Zombies) had obviously been fruitful.

Unfortunately, the album died a quick death (it wasn't even released in the UK), but on the engineering front Fisher was successful with his work for Captain Sensible, whose single "Happy Talk" became a number 1 hit in the UK.

Throughout most of the eighties Matthew Fisher became an institution in the South London music scene – there was hardly anywhere else you could go and get a world-class producer and engineer for the price of a novice. It is also characteristic of him that he gladly lent his abundant talents as a musician to anyone who entered his studio to record.

In the latter part of the eighties no new Matthew Fisher solo material was released, but a collection of demos from his private vaults came out under the title *A Salty Dog Returns*, while US label Endangered Records released a hastily-recorded CD with Fisher and members of The Downliners Sect, called *A Light Went Out In New York*.

Other members

For a couple of years after 1977 Keith Reid largely abandoned the rock business as an artist and went into management instead, working with performers such as Mickey Jupp and Frankie Miller. In 1980 he started contributing lyrics to Robin Trower and in 1983 to Gary Brooker and Matthew Fisher in connection with the *Echoes In The Night* album. Considerably less interesting for fans of Reid's old style but very commercially successful was a lyric he wrote called "You're The Voice", which became a No 1 hit for John Farnham in Australia in 1986 (UK number 6).

Procol Harum's first guitarist, Richard Brown, today lives in Northern Scotland. He is still active touring and recording, and also runs a studio.

Allan Morris, the group's first Hammond organist, apparently left the music business sometime in the late 1960s and took up working in management instead. His whereabouts today are unknown.

After being asked to leave Procol Harum in the summer of 1967 Bobby Harrison and Ray Royer formed Freedom. After about a year Royer left this line-up too, turning music into more of a hobby. Harrison meanwhile soldiered on with Freedom as a blues-rock trio. He also made a solo album, and then formed Snafu. Around 1980 Harrison moved to Iceland, where he recorded a fine blues album backed by local heroes Mezzoforte. He is currently back in Southend again and still active as a singer.

After his departure in 1969 Dave Knights turned to managing groups. However, for a brief while he was in a pop rock band called

Ruby, whose LP *Red Crystal Fantasies* (Chrysalis CHR 1061, 1974) according to Knights himself was ruined by "force of circumstance".

Guitarist *Dave Ball*, who left Procol Harum in 1972, went on to form Bedlam along with his brother Denny, drummer Cozy Powell and singer Francesco Aiello. They made one self-titled LP for Chrysalis (CHR 1046, 1973). Ball also played for a while in Long John Baldry's backing group, before moving to the USA. On returning to the UK he enlisted in the armed forces. Later, he emigrated to Australia. Today he is back in Britain, still occasionally playing guitar but mainly working in the computer industry.

Alan Cartwright left the music business altogether. Today he runs a restaurant.

Chris Copping emigrated to Australia, where he still lives and makes his living by writing music for commercial use in particular.

Following the demise of Procol Harum, guitarist Mick Grabham formed a band in his own name and made some attempts to record an LP. Gary Brooker added piano to a few tracks, but the album was never released. Grabham then joined various bands such as The Dukes and Bandit after which he resorted to session work and gradually turned his energy more towards building up a catering business. However, he is still active, playing on sessions and in groups.

Pete Solley also went more into session work and writing arrangements (he wrote the score for The Jam's "Smithers-Jones"). He now lives in the USA and runs his own company making MIDI backing-tracks.

Barrie James Wilson was auditioned for several famous groups such as AC/DC and The Who, but ended up joining Frankie Miller instead. He appeared on Miller's 1978 LP, *Double Trouble* (Chrysalis 1174). After that Wilson moved to the US and for a while became a permanent member of Joe Cocker's touring band. Sometime in the late eighties he was met with an accident and ended up in a coma for a long while.

BJ Wilson finally died on 8 October 1990. In the Procol Party Souvenir Programme, issued by *Shine On* after the group's 30th anniversary party in 1997, Wilson's lifelong friend Kenny White wrote:

"The most wonderful thing about BJ was that he was solid, he was open – you knew where you stood with him. He had a good sense of humour, he was well natured – he had his darker moments but through it all, he was a great friend. He was a gentle man and a gentleman. Nothing ever really changed – the boy I met at the beginning was the man I knew at the end."

The reunion

During all the time I have known these ex-Procol Harum members there have been constant rumours of a reunion. Only God knows how I have suffered every time they turned out to be false.

I was all the more surprised when, in the summer of 1991, I had a telephone conversation with Matthew Fisher and he exploded a bomb. It is for real now, he claimed. They were making a new record. They had Robin Trower back on guitar. They even had a tour planned in the States the following autumn.

This was the culmination of a project which had started some two years earlier, when Gary Brooker commenced work on what was then intended to become a new solo album. He called Keith Reid and asked if he was interested in some form of renewed collaboration. Reid, who was living in New York at that time, suggested Brooker come over so that they could start working together.

During one hectic week in a local studio the two of them, with producer/engineer and songwriter Matt Noble managed to write and record some four or five songs. As they were now thinking of turning the project into a Procol Harum reunion they called Matthew Fisher to hear if he was interested in joining them and assisting in the songwriting process.

Fisher was positive, and subsequently some demos were made using bass player Dave Bronze, guitarist Tim Renwick and drummer Henry Spinetti.

Following that, Robin Trower was also approached. Listening to the tapes that had been recorded so far his response was immediately positive. No fewer than four former members of the band's classic line-up were now involved, and the reunited Procol Harum had become a fact.

Normally, band reunions are difficult to handle. What are musicians supposed to do in such a situation? Play all their old hits for a couple of months and then fade back into oblivion? Or try to sound like a modern group?

Neither makes much sense. What Procol Harum did instead was make an album which sounded more-or-less as if they had never split up, but had just kept on going all through the years. It was a modern sound, but it was still very much the old group.

One important feature in particular secured the connection with the past. Throughout *The Prodigal Stranger* practically every single track has a dominant Hammond organ, just like on the very first LP twenty-five years before.

The main problem was what to do with the drumming. The role of BJ Wilson seemed impossible to fill. For a while drum machines were used, but obviously a real player was needed both on the final recordings and for "live" performances.

So Matthew Fisher asked his sons for advice, assuming they would be more in touch with the current rock scene. They suggested the band get in touch with Mark Brzezicki, who had previously been in Big Country. Brzezicki – like BJ Wilson – is an amazing drummer with a highly flamboyant and personal style. Luckily he turned out to be a long-standing fan of the group, and he soon agreed to join.

Dave Bronze stayed on bass. He had previous been with both Gary Brooker and Robin Trower. Bronze is a highly skilled player, albeit with a style considerably different from Procol Harum's original bassist, David Knights. Where Knights would always be melodic and centre his playing on more or less fixed figures, Bronze's style is founded more on grooves and rhythms. Together with Mark Brzezicki he ensured that the new Procol Harum would not just be a nostalgic trip but include a contemporary element as well.

The Prodigal Stranger has been described as the best album ever made by a re-formed sixties group. It is more than that. It is a real Procol Harum LP with a prominent scent of Bach and Brooker, of fine poetry, of blues guitar and Hammond organ from start to finish. Particularly on the lyrical front it is satisfying to note a significant progress in Reid's writing. Most of the subject matter is surprisingly positive without becoming by any means "happy-go-lucky", and at least three songs on this album, "The Hand That Rocks The Cradle", "A Dream In Every Home" and "The Pursuit Of Happiness" have about them an air of reconciliation and finding peace with the world which was never present in his early work.

The reunited Procol Harum soon found themselves touring both the US and mainland Europe. I saw them in Copenhagen in February 1992 playing to a full house. By then their guitarist was the splendid Geoff Whitehorn (ex-Crawler and Bad Company), who seemed the best possible choice since Trower had refused to go on the road with the band.

Did we all shed a tear when Brooker and Fisher started off "Homburg" together? Indeed we did! And what on earth was happening in the middle of "A Salty Dog"? I can't even say. It was *really* something magic.

Afterwards out in the street again even the cold Scandinavian winter air couldn't cut through the mist that surrounded our heads. It had really happened. The boys were back in town.

Shortly afterwards they went off to Canada to do a concert with the Edmonton Symphony Orchestra!

After the tours of 1992-94 Procol Harum mainly became an on/off project rekindled in connection with minor tours and single gigs. Perhaps their most prestigious concert of this kind was at London's Barbican with the London Symphony Orchestra in 1996.

Owing to the nature of this situation line-ups have been highly unstable. Even Matthew Fisher was out for a short while, and the concert in Edmonton was performed with Don Snow (ex-Squeeze) on organ. Drummers have included Henry Spinetti, Ian Wallace and Graham Broad. When Dave Bronze went off to play with Eric Clapton, he was replaced by Matt Pegg.

In June 1997 the *Shine On* fanzine arranged a concert at the Harlequin in Redhill, Surrey, to commemorate the thirtieth anniversary of "A Whiter Shade Of Pale". That evening they all gathered on stage in combinations the world had never heard before - Gary Brooker, Matthew Fisher, Chris Copping, Mick Grabham, Pete Solley, Alan Cartwright, Dave Bronze, Graham Broad and Matt Pegg. For a full account of this fine, memorable event look no further than Roland Clare's fine report in "The Procol Party Souvenir Programme", issued by *Shine On* shortly after.

Today Matthew Fisher has practically left the music business and works instead as a computer programmer, though it is not unlikely that he may join his old mates on stage for future one-off events.

Gary Brooker has been extremely active during the mid-nineties as a member of two bands in particular, one formed around Ringo Starr, the other around ex-Rolling Stones bass player Bill Wyman. He also appeared in the film version of *Evita* playing the role of Argentina's Defence Secretary.

In between Brooker has found time to set up his own label, Gazza Records. The first release was a recording of an "unplugged" concert held for the benefit of a small church near his home in Surrey, a very fine performance featuring both old and new material performed by group, choir and a string section.

Likewise, Robin Trower has recorded two albums in his own name, "Twentieth Century Blues" and "Someday Blues" which, as indicated in the titles, both mark a return to his original source of inspiration. He has furthermore been busy producing two excellent albums for Bryan Ferry.

This book has been an attempt to describe forty years of active musical career, and for obvious reasons such a career has its ups and downs. Reckoning up the numbers of gigs, tours and record releases in the whole career of a group like Procol Harum, with all its forerunners and offshoots, would be a truly mind-boggling task. I'm sure that past and present members of the band occasionally have to ask themselves if it was really worth the effort, the blood and sweat, the struggling, the arguments, the bitterness, depressions and sometimes crushed illusions.

All I can say is that from a long-standing fan's point of view it was all of great benefit. My life has been incomparably enriched by listening to Procol Harum records, as well as seeing the group play "live".

Best of all, I can't help feeling that there's still much more to come from this bunch of truly exceptional musicians and songwriters.

Footnotes

1   Liner-notes for *Whiter Shades Of R&B*, Edsel Records 1983
2   Procol Party Souvenir Programme, 1997.
3   Liner-notes for *Whiter Shades Of R&B*, Edsel Records 1983
4   Liner-notes for *Whiter Shades Of R&B*, Edsel Records 1983
5   From interview conducted by Henry Scott-Irvine. Published in fanzine *Shine On* April 1993 (also later in *Record Collector* No. 185).
6   Procol Party Souvenir Programme, 1997
7   Procol Party Souvenir Programme, 1997
8   Procol Party Souvenir Programme, 1997
9   *Shine On*, July 1997, Paul Carter interview
10   Tim de Lisle, *Lives Of The Great Songs*
11   *Shine On*, July 1997, Paul Carter interview
12   *Newsweek*, 31.7.67
13   Barry Miles, *Many Years From Now*
14   For more details on Guy Stevens' tumultuous career look no further than Campbell Devine's biography of Mott The Hoople, *All The Young Dudes*.
15   Both Brooker and Fisher have independently stated they are sure that this was the spelling they saw on the certificate. However, Latin experts claim that Harum is the correct form. Persistent attempts by fans to retrieve the birth certificate in question have proved fruitless.
16   Richard Williams and Mark Plummer interview, *Melody Maker* 24.3.73
17   *Zigzag* Magazine, 1976
18   *Zigzag* Magazine, 1973
19   Liner-notes for *Punk or What*, 1998

Discography

PARAMOUNTS ORIGINAL UK DISCOGRAPHY
Singles
Poison Ivy/I Feel Good All Over (Parlophone R5093, 1963)
Little Bitty Pretty One/A Certain Girl (R5107, 1964)
I'm The One Who Loves You/It Won't Be Long (R5155, 1964)
Bad Blood/Do I (R5187, 1964)
Blue Ribbons/Cuttin' In (R5752, 1965)
You Never Had It So Good/Don't You Like My Love (R5351, 1965)
EP
The Paramounts (Parlophone GEP 8908, 1964)
Compilation LP/CD
Whiter Shades Of R&B (Edsel ED 112, 1983)
The Paramounts At Abbey Road 1963-1970 (CD only, EMI 496 4362, 1998)

PROCOL HARUM ORIGINAL UK DISCOGRAPHY
Singles
* = track not on original album. ** = different mix to album version. *** = edited version.
A Whiter Shade Of Pale*/Lime Street Blues* (Deram DM 126, 1967)
Homburg*/Good Captain Clack** (Regal Zonophone RZ 3003, 1967)
Quite Rightly So**/In The Wee Small Hour Of Sixpence* (RZ 1007, 1968)
A Salty Dog**/Long Gone Geek* (RZ 3019, 1969)
Conquistador (live)/Luskus Delph (live)*(Chrysalis CHS 2003)
Robert's Box/A Rum Tale (CHS 2010, 1973)
A Souvenir Of London/Toujours l'Amour (CHS 2015, 1973)
Nothing But The Truth/Drunk Again* (CHS 2032, 1974)
Pandora's Box/The Piper's Tune (CHS 2073, 1975)
The Final Thrust***/Taking The Time (CHS 2079, 1975)
A Strong As Samson***/The Unquiet Zone (CHS 2084, 1976)
Wizard Man/Backgammon* (CHS 2183, 1977)
LPs
Procol Harum (Regal Zonophone LRZ 1001, 1967)
Shine On Brightly (Mono/Stereo LRZ/SLRZ 1004, 1968)
A Salty Dog (SLRZ 1009, 1969)
Home (w/insert, SLRZ 1014, 1970)

Live In Concert With Edmonton Orchestra (Chrysalis CR1004, 1972)
Broken Barricades (Chrysalis ILPS 9158, 1971)
Grand Hotel (w/booklet, Chrysalis CHR 1037, 1973)
Exotic Birds And Fruit (CHR 1058, 1974)
Procol's Ninth (w/lyric insert, CHR 1080, 1975)
Something Magic (CHR 1130, 1977)
The Prodigal Stranger (BMG/Zoo PL 90589, German pressing, also CD PL 90589 with lyrics)
BBC Live In Concert (Strange Fruit SFRSCD089, 1999)

SOME INTERESTING UK AND FOREIGN RELEASES
Singles
DUFFY POWER, Parchman Farm/Tired Broke And Busted (Parlophone R5111, 1964)
The Paramounts backing lead vocalist Duffy Power.
PROCOL HARUM, Quite Rightly So/Rambling On (Polydor 59 175, 1968)
Scandinavian single in picture sleeve with alternative mixes of both songs. A-side also has alternative lyrics.
PROCOL HARUM, Il Tuo Diamante/Fortuna (IL NIL 9005, 1968)
Italian single in picture sleeve. A-side is "Shine On Brightly" sung in Italian. B-side is "Repent Walpurgis".
LEGEND, Georgia George/July (Bell BLL 1082, 1969)
Procol Harum members backing Mickey Jupp.
PROCOL HARUM, Adagio/The Blue Danube (Chrysalis CHA 141, 1976)
French single only. The B-side is also available on Austrian compilation LP "In Strauss und Boden - Hommage á Johann Strauss" (Ariola 0120089, 1975).
PROCOL HARUM, The Truth Won't Fade Away/Learn To Fly/Into The Flood (Zoo/BMG PD 49160, 1991)
German CD single. "Into The Flood" is unreleased elsewhere.
LPs/CDs
VARIOUS ARTISTS, The First Great Rock Festival Of The Seventies - Isle Of Wight/Atlanta Pop Festival (CBS 66311, 1971)
Triple LP including Procol Harum doing "A Salty Dog" in concert.
PROCOL HARUM, Procol Harum Lives (A&M SP 8053, US promo, 1970s)

15 min. interview from April 1971 including Procol Harum singing "Maybe It's Because I'm A Londoner".

PROCOL HARUM, The Best Of Procol Harum (Fly TON 4, 1970s)
UK compilation including real stereo mixes of "Homburg", "She Wandered Through The Garden Fence" and "Conquistador". These tracks are also featured on several compilation CDs.

PROCOL HARUM, The Best Of Procol Harum (A&M SP-4401, 1970s)
US compilation including alternative version of "In The Wee Small Hours Of Sixpence", reputedly with Bobby Harrison on drums. This track is also featured on several compilation CDs.

VARIOUS ARTISTS, Over The Rainbow (CHR 1079, 1975)
Includes "live" versions of "Grand Hotel" and Procol Harum backing Frankie Miller on "Brickyard Blues".

PROCOL HARUM, Rock Roots (Fly Roots 4, late 1970s)
Includes two previously unissued songs, "Seem To Have The Blues (Most All Of The Time)" and "Monsieur Armand". "Conquistador" has different organ solo to LP original. These tracks are also featured on several compilation CDs.

PROCOL HARUM, Retro Rock (no catalogue number, 1982)
US radio station promo featuring Procol Harum recorded "live" in 1973 with the Los Angeles Philharmonic Orchestra.

PROCOL HARUM, The Return of Procol Harum (Zoo ZP17044-2, 1991)
Promo only US interview CD.

PROCOL HARUM, The Prodigal Stranger (BVCP-158, 1991)
Japanese CD issue. Includes otherwise unavailable version of "Man With A Mission" with guitar solo.

VARIOUS ARTISTS, The Symphonic Music Of Procol Harum (BMG 09026-68029-2, 1995)
CD only US release featuring the London Symphony Orchestra backing different artists performing Procol Harum songs. With contributions from Gary Brooker, Robin Trower, Matthew Fisher, Dave Bronze, Mark Brzezicki and Geoff Whitehorn.

GARY BROOKER SOLO UK DISCOGRAPHY
Singles
* = track not on original album.

Savannah/S.S. Blues* (P/S, Chrysalis CHS 2326, 1979)
Say It Ain't So Joe/Angelina (P/S, CHS 2347, 1979)
Leave The Candle*/Chasing The Chop* (CHS 2396, 1980)
Homelovin'/Chasing For The Chop (alt.)* (P/S Mercury MER 70, 1981)
The Cycle (Let It Flow)/Badlands* (P/S MER 94, 1982)
The Long Goodbye/Trick Of The Night (P/S MER 181, 1984)
Two Fools In Love/Summer Nights* (P/S MER 188, 1985)
LPs/CDs
No More Fear Of Flying (Chrysalis CHR 1224, 1979)
Lead Me To The Water (Mercury 6359 098, 1982)
Echoes In The Night (Mercury MERL 68/also CD 824 652-2, 1985)

MATTHEW FISHER SOLO DISCOGRAPHY
LPs/CDs
Journey's End (RCA SF 8380, 1983)
I'll Be There (RCA APL1 0352, 1974)
Matthew Fisher (Vertigo 9198 652, 1980)
Strange Days (Dutch Mercury 6302 108, 1981)
A Salty Dog Returns (CD only, Promised Land 112152, 1990)
A Light Went Out In New York (credited to "Matthew Fisher And The Downliners Sect", CD only, US, Endangered Records AD69, 1993)
For copies of "A Light Went Out In New York" write to: Endangered Records, 4 Daniels Farm Road, Suite 104, Trumbull, CT 06611, USA.

ROBIN TROWER UK DISCOGRAPHY
Singles
* = track not on original album.
Man Of The World/Take A Fast Train* (Chrysalis CHS 2009, 1973)
Too Rolling Stoned/Lady Love (CHS 2046, 1974)
Caledonia/Messin' The Blues (CHS 2124, 1976)
It's For You/My Love/In City Dreams (P/S, some on red vinyl, CHS 2247, 1978)
It's For You/My Love (P/S CHS 2256, 1978)
Victims Of The Fury/One In A Million* (CHS 2402, 1980)
Jack And Jill/The Shout (CHS 2423, 1980)
What It Is/Into Money (P/S, some clear vinyl, CHS 2497, 1981)

LPs/CDs
Twice Removed From Yesterday (Chrysalis CHR 1039, 1973)
Bridge Of Sighs (CHR 1057, 1974)
For Earth Below (CHR 1073, 1975)
Robin Trower Live (CHR 1089, 1976)
Long Misty Days (CHR 1107, 1976)
In City Dreams (CHR 1148, 1977)
Caravan To Midnight (CHR 1189, 1978)
Victims Of The Fury (CHR 1215, 1980)
B.L.T. (credited to B.L.T., CHR 1324, 1981)
Truce (credited to Robin Trower & Jack Bruce, CHR 1352, 1982)
Back It Up (CHR 1420, 1983)
Beyond The Mist (Music For Nations MFN 51, 1985)
Passion (PRT N6563, 1987)
Take What You Need (Atlantic LP/CD 781 838-1/781 838-2, 1988)
BBC Live In Concert (Windsong WINDCD 013, CD only, 1992)
20th Century Blues (Demon FIENDCD 753, CD only, 1994)
Someday Blues (Demon FIENDCD 931, CD only, 1997)
Live On The King Bisquit Flower Hour (KBFHCD 020, CD only, recorded 1977, released 1998)

MICK GRABHAM PRE-PROCOL HARUM UK DISCOGRA-PHY
Singles
PLASTIC PENNY, Nobody Knows It/Happy Just To Be With You (Page One POF 062, 1968)
PLASTIC PENNY, Your Way To Tell Me Go/Baby You're Not To Blame (POF 079, 1968)
PLASTIC PENNY, Hound Dog/Currency (POF 107, 1969)
PLASTIC PENNY, She Does/Genevieve (POF 146, 1969)
COCHISE, Watch This Space/59th St. Bridge Song (United Artists UP 35134, 1970)
COCHISE, Love's Made A Fool Of You/Words Of A Dying Man (Liberty LBS 15425, 1970)
COCHISE, Why I Sing The Blues/Jed Colider (LBF 15460, 1971)
MICK GRABHAM SOLO, On Fire For You Baby/Sweet Blossom Woman (United Artists UP 35391, 1972)
LPs

PLASTIC PENNY, Two Sides Of The Penny (Page One POL(S) 005, 1968)

PLASTIC PENNY, Currency (POLS 014, 1969)

PLASTIC PENNY, Heads You Win, Tails I Loose (POS 611, 1070)

COCHISE, Swallow Tales (Liberty LBS 83428, 1970)

COCHISE, Cochise (United Artists 29117, 1971)

COCHISE, So Far (United Artists UAS 29286, 1972)

MICK GRABHAM SOLO, Mick The Lad (United Artists UAS 29341, 1972)

CURRENT CD REISSUES
Procol Harum CDs on Westside
All Westside CD reissues include rare/unreleased material and sleeve-notes by Henry Scott-Irvine.

30th Anniversary Anthology (3-CD, WESX 301)

1st Album ... Plus! (WESM 527)

Shine On Brightly ... Plus! (UK sleeve, WESM 553)

A Salty Dog ... Plus! (WESM 534)

Home ... Plus! (WESM 535)

Repertoire Procol Harum and related CDs
Repertoire are a German label. All their CD reissues except "Home" include rare material, have sleeve-notes by Chris Welch and are digi-packs.

GARY BROOKER, No More Fear Of Flying (REP 4659)

THE GARY BROOKER ENSEMBLE, Within Our House (REP 4660)

PROCOL HARUM, A Whiter Shade Of Pale (REP 4666-WY)

PROCOL HARUM, Shine On Brightly (US sleeve, REP 4667-WY)

PROCOL HARUM, A Salty Dog (REP 4668-WY)

PROCOL HARUM, Home (REP 4669-WY)

Procol Harum CDs on Castle
Castle have reissued the following four Procol Harum albums on CD with sleeve-notes by Henry Scott-Irvine. They are all straightforward issues except ESM 291, which includes the B-side "Drunk Again". There are currently no UK CD issues of "Broken Barricades" and "Live".

Grand Hotel (ESM CD 290)

Exotic Birds And Fruit (ESM CD 291)

Procol's Ninth (ESM CD 292)
Something Magic (ESM CD 293)

Procol Harum related CDs on BGO

Beat Goes On (BGO) are a UK label specialising in 2-on-1 releases (two original vinyl albums on one CD). They don't add bonus tracks but sound quality is very high and all include sleeve-notes.

MATTHEW FISHER, Matthew Fisher/Strange Days (BGOCD308)

ROBIN TROWER, Twice Removed From Yesterday/Bridge Of Sighs (BGOCD339)

ROBIN TROWER, For Earth Below/Live (BGOCD347)

ROBIN TROWER, Long Misty Days/In City Dreams (BGOCD349)

ROBIN TROWER, Caravan To Midnight/Victim Of The Fury (BGOCD352)

ROBIN TROWER, B.L.T./Truce (BGOCD411)

ROBIN TROWER, Back It Up (BGOCD426)

BGO have also reissued Bobby Bland's "Two Steps From The Blues" (BGOCD 163), a crucial influence on The Paramounts. Write to: Beat Goes On Records, P.O. Box 22, Bury St. Edmunds, Suffolk, EP28 6XQ, England.

Procol Harum related CDs on Angel Air

Angel Air is a UK label devoted to issuing previously-released as well as unreleased material. All their CDs include bonus material and sleeve-notes.

THE GUITAR ORCHESTRA (w/Mick Grabham), Guitar Orchestra (SJPCD002)

BOBBY HARRISON, Solid Silver (SJPCD011)

MICK GRABHAM, Mick The Lad (SJPCD012)

FREEDOM (Bobby Harrison/Ray Royer), Black On White (SJPCD028)

SNAFU (Bobby Harrison/Pete Solley), Snafu/Situation Normal (2-CD, SJPCD030)

For Angel Air and most other CD releases in this discography write to: CeeDee Mail, PO Box 14, Stowmarket, IP14 4UD, England.

Procol Harum related CDs on Gazza

THE GARY BROOKER ENSEMBLE, Within Our House (Gazza 001, 1996)

LIQUORICE JOHN DEATH, Ain't Nothing To Get Excited About (002, 1998)

Gazza releases are available through the Procol Harum newsletter, Shine On.

Procol Harum Website Address:

http://www.procolharum.com

Procol Harum newsletter "Shine On":

56 Brecknock Road, London N7 0DD

Index

Titles from SAF Publishing Ltd

No More Mr Nice Guy: The Inside Story of The Alice Cooper Group
By Michael Bruce and Billy James (reprint due soon). The dead babies, the drinking, executions and, of course, the rock 'n' roll.

Beyond The Pale: The Story of Procol Harum UK Price £12.99
Distinctive, ground breaking and enigmatic British band from the 60s.

An American Band: A History of Grand Funk Railroad UK Price £12.99
One of the biggest grossing US rock 'n' roll acts of the 70s - selling millions of records and playing sold out arenas the world over. Hype, Politics & rock 'n' roll - unbeatable!

Wish The World Away: Mark Eitzel and American Music Club UK Price £12.99
Sean Body has written a fascinating biography of Eitzel which portrays an artist tortured by demons, yet redeemed by the aching beauty of his songs.

Ginger Geezer: Vivian Stanshall & the Bonzo Dog Band (available 2000)
Stanshall was one of pop music's true eccentrics. An account of his incredible life from playing pranks with The Who's Keith Moon to depression, alcoholism, & sad demise.

Go Ahead John!: The Music of John McLaughlin UK Price £12.99
One of the greatest jazz musicians of all time. Includes his work with Miles Davis, Mahavishnu Orchestra, Shakti. Full of insights into all stages of his career.

Lunar Notes: Zoot Horn Rollo's Captain Beefheart Experience UK Price £11.95
For the first time we get the insider's story of what it was like to record, play and live with an eccentric genius such as Beefheart, written by Bill Harkleroad - Zoot himself!

Meet The Residents: America's Most Eccentric Band UK Price £11.95
An outsider's view of The Residents' operations, exposing a world where nothing is as it seems. It is a fascinating tale of musical anarchy and cartoon wackiness. Reprinted to coincide with the recent world tour.

Digital Gothic: A Critical Discography of Tangerine Dream UK Price £9.95
For the very first time German electronic pioneers, Tangerine Dream mammoth output is placed within an ordered perspective.

The One and Only - Homme Fatale: Peter Perrett & The Only Ones UK Price £11.95
An extraordinary journey through crime, punishment and the decadent times of British punk band leader, Peter Perrett of The Only Ones

Plunderphonics, 'Pataphysics and Pop Mechanics The Leading Exponents of Musique Actuelle UK Price £12.95
Chris Cutler, Fred Frith, Henry Threadgill, John Oswald, John Zorn, etc.

Kraftwerk: Man, Machine and Music UK Price £11.95
The full story behind one of the most influential bands in the history of rock.

Wrong Movements: A Robert Wyatt History UK Price £14.95
A journey through Wyatt's 30 year career with Soft Machine, Matching Mole & solo artist.

Wire: Everybody Loves A History UK Price £9.95
One of British punk's most endearing and enduring bands combining Art and Attitude

Tape Delay: A Documentary of Industrial Music (out of print)
Marc Almond, Cabaret Voltaire, Nick Cave, Chris & Cosey, Coil, Foetus, Neubauten, Non, The Fall, New Order, Psychic TV, Rollins, Sonic Youth, Swans, Test Dept and many more...

Dark Entries: Bauhaus and Beyond UK Price £11.95
The gothic rise & fall of Bauhaus, Love & Rockets, Tones on Tail, Murphy, J, and Ash solo.